Drivers of Corruption

Drivers of Corruption
A Brief Review

Tina Søreide

WORLD BANK GROUP

Contents

Foreword

Corruption represents a major obstacle to development, growth, and the effective functioning of the rule of law. Corrupt practices by public officials affect the legitimacy of offices and institutions. Furthermore, accountable political leadership cannot flourish in corrupt environments. From an economic standpoint, corruption distorts capital flows from their intended purpose and thus depletes national wealth. It reduces the impact of development assistance and provides an incentive to exploit natural resources, further depleting our environmental assets. Also, it distorts competition, spurs inequality, erodes macroeconomic stability, and hinders the development of fair market structures; it reduces the effectiveness of public administration and distorts public expenditure decisions by channeling resources to corruption-prone sectors or to personal enrichment. From a sociopolitical point of view, corruption reverses the principles of trust on which democratic systems are founded; it harms the reputation of the state, its institutions, and its leadership; it hinders the development of a strong civil society. The "cancer of corruption" undermines efforts to combat poverty and wastes the scarce resources of the international aid community.

For many years, corruption was seen as primarily, if not exclusively, a political problem with little or no relevance to economic development. Moreover, work on corruption was felt to contravene the "political prohibition" that is hardwired into the constituent documents of most (but not all) international financial institutions (IFIs), barring them from interfering in the political affairs of their members. Recently, however, the nexus between corruption and governance issues, on the one hand, and development, including economic development, on the other, has become clear. It has also become clear that, if done right, governance issues may be addressed without violating the political prohibition.

Along with this evolution in their understanding of corruption as a development issue, the IFIs have developed legal and policy frameworks to deal with corruption in their operations. The World Bank, for example, has issued Anti-Corruption Guidelines that apply to all of its investment project and program-for-results financing and has included anticorruption provisions in its General Conditions, Procurement Guidelines, and Consultant Guidelines. It has also developed an administrative system to sanction firms and individuals who are found to have engaged in corruption in connection with Bank financing.

Against this background, the World Bank, the African Development Bank, the Nordic Investment Bank, and other multilateral and bilateral development partners with a stake in the fight against corruption, including the United Nations and regional organizations such as the Organisation for Economic Co-operation and Development, academia, and research institutes, have launched a study (the Study) under the auspices of the Global Forum on Law, Justice, and Development, a mechanism shared by a worldwide network of stakeholders designed to capture, co-generate, exchange, and disseminate innovative legal solutions for development. The Study aims to understand how the opportunities and incentives for corruption—in other words, "drivers"—play out in IFI-funded operations, reflecting on the lessons this knowledge may hold for the IFIs' legal and policy frameworks for fighting corruption. To what extent does the framework address the relevant opportunities and incentives? Does it do so in the optimal manner, given what we know about those opportunities and incentives? How could that framework be adjusted to enhance its impact? In short, does what we know about corruption and what we do about it match?

This review, prepared by Dr. Tina Søreide, sets out the knowledge already generated by scholars and practitioners on the underlying opportunities and incentives for corruption. In doing so, it lays the essential foundation on which our further work can build. We are enormously grateful for Dr. Søreide's work. She has done a masterful job in bringing together the wide-ranging knowledge on this topic from disparate sources into a clear and—given its scope—concise overview, together with a rich bibliography that will allow the study to look deeper into those areas most relevant for our operations. But beyond these immediate purposes, we are confident that this lucid and informative paper is destined to become essential reading for anyone interested in a tour d'horizon of the drivers of corruption.

Hassane Cissé
Deputy General Counsel
Knowledge and Research

Acknowledgments

This review was led by Tina Søreide, an economist in the Faculty of Law, University of Bergen (Norway), and Chr. Michelsen Institute (Norway). This text was prepared for policy dialogue in the Global Forum on Law, Justice, and Development and further developed as part of the author's research on corruption. The World Bank cannot be held responsible for any flaws or statements presented. The views expressed in this paper are those of the author and do not necessarily reflect the views of the Board of Executive Directors of the World Bank or the governments they represent, and are not necessarily shared by staff of the World Bank or its management. The author thanks Emmanuelle Auriol, Lisa Bhansali, Nicola Bonucci, Shannon Bullock, Steven Burgess, Hassane Cissé, Stephan Eggli, Luis Franceschi, Athanasios Gromitsaris, Mamta Kaushal, Michael Kramer, Yasutomo Morigiwa, Nigel Quinney, Christina Stenvall-Kekkonen, and Paul Wade. The author especially thanks Frank Fariello, Susan Rose-Ackerman, and Giovanni Bo for their useful comments. Responsibility for errors or omissions remains solely with the author.

Publication of this review was made possible with support from the African Development Bank in the framework of the Global Forum on Law, Justice, and Development.

Abbreviations

BBC   British Broadcasting Corporation
CPI   Corruption Perceptions Index
FATF   Financial Action Task Force
FCPA   Foreign Corrupt Practices Act
GDP   gross domestic product
IFI   international financial institution
NGO   nongovernmental organization
OECD   Organisation for Economic Co-operation and Development
PFM   public financial management
PPP   public-private partnership
SEC   Securities and Exchange Commission
StAR   Stolen Asset Recovery Initiative

CHAPTER 1

Introduction

In the context of an organization, the word *corruption* refers to how individuals entrusted with authority to make decisions on behalf of the organization misuse their position for personal gain. Corruption occurs in both public and private organizations. It can be understood as a decision "sold" to benefit the briber, while the bribe payment compensates for the decision maker's risks and moral cost of betraying the institution. The "bought" decision deviates from what the institution would otherwise have decided (if not, there would be no reason to pay a bribe). Directly or indirectly, such corrupt decisions distort governance and bureaucratic administration—and hinder development. Corruption is often encouraged by those who benefit from distorted decisions—the bribers—and both the bribers and the officials who accept the bribes are responsible for the consequences.[1]

Corruption can take a variety of forms (see table 1.1 for a glossary). In many settings, it resembles extortion, where a party is forced to offer something of value to an individual who holds a position of authority. Extra payment is requested for public services and decisions, and this adds an informal tax on citizens and firms. These "taxes" are often unpredictable, obstruct business operations, and prevent individuals from benefiting fully from the services.[2] The damage caused by corruption in any setting depends on the mechanisms at play and the scale of the crime. The more distorted that decision-making processes become and the higher the burden of unpredictable costs on firms and individuals, the more damaging is the corruption.[3]

Corruption is difficult to combat and control. In a public setting, efficient state administration requires delegation of authority. Civil servants must be trusted to make decisions in light of multiple concerns. With discretionary authority, there will be temptations and opportunities to let personal interests make precedence over what may be best for society. In the private sector, owners and executive business leaders must let individuals represent the firm. Supervision and control are important, but there are limits to how much one can and should monitor staff members. Not only is strict control expensive,[4] it can easily be seen as a sign of low trust that may suppress motivation and accountability.

Table 1.1 Glossary of Corruption

Crony capitalism	Success in business that depends on close relationships between business people, government officials, and politicians. It is associated with favoritism in the distribution of legal permits, government grants, special tax breaks, and other forms of state intervention. When it characterizes government institutions, it is also called *kleptocracy*.
Embezzlement	Stealing state funds entails the misuse of public authority, yet strictly speaking it is not corruption. Embezzlement of state funds (that is, theft) is sometimes facilitated by corruption, but can occur in the absence of corruption. When the supply of public services is restricted with the intention of securing bribe payments (that is, some form of extortion), it is sometimes called *corruption with theft,* and this blurs the distinction between embezzlement and corruption.
Extortion/extortive corruption	Demand for a bribe payment in exchange for a decision by a government institution that makes possible a service, license, or approval otherwise offered free of charge or at low cost. It can also refer to a bribe demanded in exchange for the "opportunity" to avoid an undeserved disadvantage, such as paying a fine, even if no offense has been committed.
Facilitation payments	Extra payment for services that should be offered free of charge or at low cost. The distinction between a facilitation payment and extortion, though blurred, depends on the circumstances. In contrast to extortion, a facilitation payment may serve as an informal price that clears the market (that is, it makes the supply of services fit the demand, given users' willingness to pay). However, compared with a formal price, it will usually cause distortions because its informal character will often make the size of the price unpredictable. The degree of distortions will also depend on how substantial the additional costs are in the personal economy of most clients.
Kickback	Payment made secretively to a buyer or seller who has directed a contract or facilitated a transaction or appointment illicitly. It can also refer to the way a person in a supervisory position takes a portion of a worker's wage in return for a certain benefit, as when a supervisor arranges for a worker to get a job.
Kleptocracy	An informal system of governance in which state institutions are controlled by a network of allies who use their authority to increase their personal wealth and political power at the expense of the wider population. The term is associated with substantial embezzlement of state funds and unfair allocation of government-controlled contracts and rights.
Lobbyism/campaign finance	Refers to the act of attempting to influence decisions made by officials in the government, most often legislators or members of regulatory agencies. When combined with payments to political parties, it is called *campaign finance.* Lobbying is legal; it is not a form of corruption.
Patronage	Civil servants and politicians who, when exercising their authority, favor ethnic groups, relatives, or citizens from the same area of the country, instead of acting neutrally, as formal rules prescribe. Such corruption is not necessarily motivated by greed; often, it expresses low recognition of formal state structures and loyalty to allies.
Queue corruption	Bribes offered for a better position in the waiting line. It causes unfair allocation of rights, such as in accessing health services or obtaining some form of license.
Regulatory capture	The act of advancing the commercial or other special concerns of a particular interest group by a regulatory agency charged with regulating the industry or sector within which that interest group operates. Agencies acting under such circumstances are called *captured agencies.*
Rent-seeking	Obtaining "non-produced inputs or advantages," that is, economic rents, such as those gained by market distortions created by a regulatory agency. The term refers to efforts to manipulate the social or political environment to obtain such benefits, rather than investing time and/or money in productive work and creating new wealth thereby.
State capture	A form of political corruption in which a private interest significantly influences a state's decision-making processes to gain an advantage through illicit and nonobvious channels. Although similar to *regulatory capture*, it differs because of the wider variety of bodies through which it may be exercised.

table continues next page

Table 1.1 Glossary of Corruption *(continued)*

Systemic corruption	Corruption so prevalent that it is part of the everyday structure of society. It reflects substantial institutional weaknesses, not just the integrity flaws of some individuals. When the consequences of working against corruption are too high for individuals, and even managers, in government institutions, they adapt, rather than react to the situation.
Tender corruption	Bribes offered to influence the outcome of competition for public procurement contracts. Bribery involved in government contracting is not associated exclusively with bidding; it can also take place at the planning/budgeting stage or agreed to before the tender and later combined with renegotiated contracts or flawed quality controls. It sometimes facilitates cartel collaboration.

Source: This glossary is based on various dictionaries and databases on the Web, including the Free Dictionary.com, Ask.com, and Merriam-Webster.com.

Yet, it is difficult to control firms' and citizens' propensity to influence decision makers. A bribe payment is typically made in the decision maker's "personal economy" (that is, his or her personal financial situation); the bribe may be small compared with the public value affected, but even a small amount can be substantial to the decision maker. Decisions bought (informally) at a low price compared with the (official) values at stake imply potentially huge net benefits for the briber. Given the difficulties of controlling each and every bureaucratic decision and the potential importance of even small values to the bribe recipient's personal economy, it is nearly impossible to eradicate the risk of corruption. In short, the risk of corruption is an inevitable side effect of efficient bureaucratic organization.

A state institution can be trustworthy even when sporadic corruption exists. An occasional corruption case may simply indicate that a control system, audit, or whistle-blower channel is working. How "healthy" an institution is depends on how a case is handled when corruption is revealed; an institution may have several cases of corruption over, say, a decade, and still perform well. In a "less healthy" institution, the corruption might be allowed to continue.

Some of the most common integrity mechanisms vis-à-vis government institutions are listed in table 1.2. Horizontally, a distinction is made between administrative governance and the political level. Vertically, a distinction is made

Table 1.2 Legal Approaches for Preventing and Disclosing Corruption and Protecting Fair Competition in Markets

	Legal approaches	
Undue influence/corruption	*Prevention mechanism*	*Disclosure mechanism*
State administration and industry regulation	Criminalization of corruption; impartiality requirements; codes of conduct; competition laws; procurement rules; employer liability	Investigation/criminal law processes; audits; leniency; financial control of taxes/income; whistle-blower protection; confidentiality rules; access-to-information laws
The political level and government ministries	Impartiality requirements; bureaucratic control over government proposals (internal); public lobby registers; independent sector regulation	Constitutional checks and balances; financial control of taxes/income; media; watchdogs; whistle-blowers; auditors

Source: Adapted from Søreide (2011).

Drivers of Corruption • http://dx.doi.org/10.1596/978-1-4648-0401-4

between mechanisms to prevent corruption and mechanisms to disclose corruption. Understanding how these work for different sectors and parts of a society is an important first step in assessing the risks of corruption.

Regardless of how corruption is estimated, there is huge variation in the extent of corruption across countries, due mostly to variations in institutional quality and political accountability. Despite data weaknesses, one can see fairly robust correlations between income levels and corruption, and developing countries are generally more affected by corruption than are the more developed countries that are members of the Organisation for Economic Co-operation and Development (OECD).

The panels in figure 1.1 confirm these patterns. They also show that a substantial proportion of firms (36.8 percent of 135,000 firms surveyed) consider

Figure 1.1 Regional Experiences with Corruption

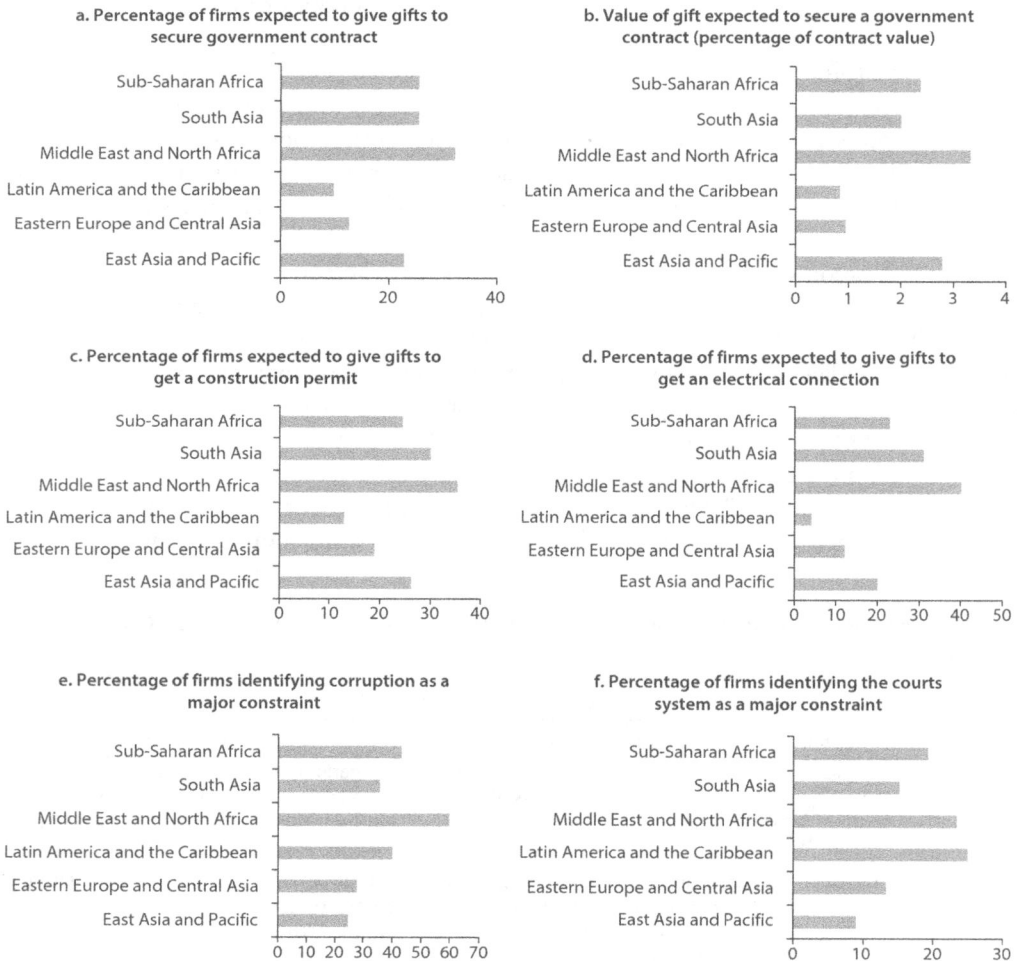

Source: World Bank Enterprises Survey, http://www.enterprisesurveys.org.

corruption "a major constraint" to business operations. Panel *e* in figure 1.1. indicates that as many as 60 percent of firms in the Middle East and North Africa see corruption as an obstacle. At the world average, more than 18 percent of firms surveyed consider the court system a problem, meaning they cannot trust that their contracts and other rights will be respected. At the world average, more than 20 percent of firms expect that they have to give gifts to obtain a construction permit. The word "gift" has different meanings, of course, but even if only half of these gifts are considered as bribes, the figure is still depressingly high. Corruption has a range of consequences, but just the market impediments indicated by these graphs would likely hamper development significantly.

Too frequently, and possibly due to the oversimplified cross-country rankings of the problem, corruption is referred to as *one* phenomenon. In reality, there are different forms of corruption, and the world map of perceived corruption levels[5] can look different depending on what form of corruption is being considered. According to Auriol (2014), *collusive* corruption—referring to deals planned by both parties and from which both parties benefit—is a worldwide challenge (see box 2.1), while *extortive* corruption—when the ones who pay the bribe feels compelled to do so—occurs mostly in developing countries. The latter form of corruption is easier to classify as illegal and is better captured by perception-based corruption indices.[6] In cases of collusive corruption, those involved collaborate to create the perception that all rules and procedures have been respected, which makes the crime much more difficult to control.

Certain characteristics make some markets and government institutions more exposed to corruption than others, including market players' organizational features and cultures, financial arrangements, ownership structures, and home country origins.[7] A case of corruption must not only be seen as an act by individuals who have decided to commit the crime but also be understood to be a result of context and "framework conditions" (that is, the external factors relevant to an individual's decision that the individual cannot influence). Characteristics of a given country; its political situation; its society, history, and norms; institutional qualities; a given setting; and the cast of players provide "layers of explanatory factors."

Academic disciplines place different weight on these "layers" and therefore tend to explain corruption differently. These differences are mirrored in policy recommendations. Economists typically address the incentives of the individuals involved or the profit-maximizing strategies of firms, although framework conditions are obviously important in terms of determining the expected outcomes of alternative options. Psychologists and behavioral scientists add nuance to economic theories by explaining the limits of human rationality, an approach that is relevant to understanding a phenomenon such as corruption. Anthropologists and sociologists typically address how framework conditions and history shape cultural norms and individual assessments of right and wrong. Political scientists tend to describe the mechanics of the larger governance system, including functional weaknesses in checks and balances and various power games.[8] The conditions for holding players responsible are addressed primarily by the legal discipline.[9]

Many academics will agree, however, that it makes sense to consider how well policy initiatives address the causes of corruption, particularly because there is limited (solid) evidence on what works to combat corruption. This report draws on several branches of the literature in an attempt to explain those causes, or *drivers*, of corruption.[10] Chapter 2 describes the arenas for corruption; that is, the circumstances where control over assets is particularly exposed to corrupt influences. Chapter 3 discusses the individual's propensity to exploit the opportunities for corruption that exist, as well as the question of why corruption does not necessarily elicit a response even when it is observed. Both aspects are crucial to understanding why corruption persists; and, generally, understanding the different layers of corruption risks is important when designing an effective anticorruption strategy. Chapter 4 lists implications for policy debate and research.

The report concludes that it is possible to develop efficient policy mechanisms and control the problem—*if* the international community understands the consequences of corruption and is equipped with insights about the sources of context-specific values achievable through corruption, the individual propensity to grab, and the moral environment. Political corruption, weak state legitimacy, and fragile state structures impede efficient reform; efficient solutions must therefore often involve international players. Lack of political will is not only a developing country concern, however. In all categories of countries, anticorruption progress is being pushed by international collaboration, and the ability to control the most entrenched corruption depends on the willingness of governments in the most developed economies to participate with developing countries in anticorruption campaigns. Collaboration between policy makers and researchers contributes not only to better institutional solutions but also, and increasingly, to better understanding of the dynamics of anticorruption reform at the micro and macro decision-making levels.

Notes

1. The Joint International Financial Institutions (IFI) Task Force Against Corruption defines corruption in its task force note from 2006 as "the offering, giving, receiving, or soliciting, directly or indirectly, anything of value to influence improperly the actions of another party." See World Bank (2012). For examples of corruption cases, see the website of the US Securities and Exchange Commission; Transparency International's *Daily Corruption News*; the *FCPA Blog* (http://fcpablog.com); the "FCPA Map" prepared by Mintz Group (http://fcpamap.com/); and the World Bank website (press releases by the Integrity Vice Presidency), among other sources.

2. See Méon and Sekkat (2005) for empirical analysis. De Soto (1989) presents a case study from Peru.

3. Different academic views about corruption as a cause or consequence of other dysfunctions in society have led to different policy perspectives. Susan Rose-Ackerman (2010b) explains that those with a more libertarian view may consider corruption an efficient strategy to bypass cost-imposing and rigid state regulations. A more ethnographic view on society might defend corruption as a cultural norm. Macroeconomic results, however, are very clear about the negative relationship between corruption

and economic development. See, among others, Svensson (2005), Kaufmann (2003), and Aidt (2011). Lambsdorff (2006), Treisman (2007), and Rose-Ackerman and Truex (2013) provide useful literature reviews.

4. The marginal benefit of control decreases in the extent of control, which means that more control makes economic sense only up to a certain point (where marginal returns of control equal its marginal costs). See Rose-Ackerman (2010a).

5. Consider, for example, the best-known map of perceived corruption levels, that published yearly by Transparency International.

6. Auriol (2014) applies data from the World Bank Enterprise Surveys. The firms' responses confirm her theory of more extortive corruption reported for developing countries and "capture forms of corruption" in all categories of countries, with a far weaker distinction between developing countries and developed economies. For a recent presentation of corruption risks in OECD countries, see, for example, the EU 2014 Anti-Corruption Report (3.2.2014: COM(2014) 38 final), available at http://ec.europa.eu/dgs/home-affairs/what-we-do/policies/organized-crime-and-human-trafficking/corruption/anti-corruption-report/index_en.htm.

7. Exposed sectors include utilities, construction, extractive industries, aid, and defense. Sector challenges are described in Campos and Pradhan (2007) and Søreide and Williams (2014), and in numerous sector reviews available on the Internet. See the websites of the U4 Anti-Corruption Resource Center and Transparency International: http://www.u4.no/ and http://www.transparency.org/.

8. See, among others, chapters in Heidenheimer and Johnson (2002), Kunicova (2006), and Rose and Heywood (2013).

9. This report includes references from all of these disciplines, but is colored by the author's background as an economist.

10. This survey does not include all results. For more comprehensive reviews, see Rose-Ackerman (1999), Heidenheimer and Johnston (2002), Abed and Gupta (2002), and Lambsdorff (2007).

CHAPTER 2

Arenas for Corruption: Access to Assets

Corruption is motivated by the possibility of securing something of value for oneself and one's allies. The desire to secure benefits is a human trait and generally positive for development; various forms of rewards drive humans to get up in the morning, do a good job, and act responsibly. The discussion now turns to the opportunity to secure more benefits than one is entitled to within the existing "rules of the game"; specifically, the opportunity to *grab* at the expense of society.[1]

A decision maker has the authority to influence an outcome that matters to the briber. For steering a decision in the briber's direction, the decision maker is compensated with a bribe. The steered decision and the bribe now become assets that usually exceed what at least one of the players would have obtained without the corrupt act. The opportunity to seize assets through some form of power misuse differs across sectors, organizations, and decision-making situations. This chapter describes the circumstances in which the risk of corruption is particularly high—in other words, where the *drivers of corruption* can be found.

Shortage and Illegality

There is risk of corruption whenever someone has discretionary authority to influence others' framework conditions. The mechanisms at play depend on the specific authority and the benefits that may be obtained. If an extra price (a bribe) is demanded for a service provided free or at low price, the extra charge is a form of theft. The amounts (or rents) accruing to the civil servant who makes such demands can be significant, even if the extra payment made by each client is low. If combined with some form of extortion (that is, "you don't get what you want unless you pay"), the price/bribe will depend on how highly the client values the service or benefit. A client in urgent need of hospital services, for example, may have a high willingness to pay. As in other markets, the size of the payment increases if demand is higher than supply. A civil servant who has the power to create some form of shortage will easily make the corruption more rewarding by controlling supply.[2] For example, regardless of the capacity at a port, a customs official may deny a user the right to offload goods in the absence of a substantial payment.[3] Receiving a driver's license may depend on the willingness to bribe, instead of the driver's demonstrated competence.[4] A teacher may create a shortage of good grades by keeping the best grades for those who pay informally, regardless of how well-qualified a student is.[5] The allocation of public contracts is typically in shortage because of the private sector's demand for contracts, but an influential civil servant can create further shortage by excluding suppliers that are not willing to pay bribes.[6]

Illegality is another aspect of corruption that easily increases the size of assets available for grabbing. Civil servants know that criminals are more likely to commit a crime if there is a public administrator—a police officer, for example—who can make sure the crime will go unnoticed or actively facilitate the crime. In this case, the civil servant gains a portion of the criminal returns, such as the sale of drugs, weapons, or other illegal goods or services, with the size of the portion based on the decisions offered.[7] Accordingly, corruption is typically higher in areas with high levels of crime, particularly crime related to the Mafia, cartel market collaboration, and tax evasion.[8] A frightening fact is that even the support needed to prepare a terrorist attack can be bought if the price is high enough.[9]

It is important to understand how the characteristics of decisions that are offered in exchange for a bribe determine the size of the bribe. Regardless of sector, level of decision making, and legal status of the assets, returns from corruption will usually be higher for the decision maker who is more capable of controlling supply of some sort and exposing clients to extortion; that is, services that can be held back until a bribe is paid. The briber's willingness to pay—for securing an important contract or receiving life-saving medical treatment, for example—is another factor that can increase the size of bribes. Circumstances in which the net benefit of corruption is particularly high must be understood as drivers of corruption.[10]

Organization of State Authority

The opportunity to demand bribes, increase their size through a more or less artificially induced shortage, and/or exploit clients' willingness to pay all depend crucially on civil servants' authority and how bureaucracies are organized. In some countries, state authority itself may be seen as a tool for grabbing, especially in fragile, postconflict states and in countries where state structures are perceived as imposed, rather than the result of a unified demand from citizens. The premise of a functioning state implies allocation of authority, and authority, in turn, is particularly exposed to misuse when control functions are weak; citizens are illiterate, disorganized, or uninformed about what they should expect; and those in power use corruption to establish a network of allies in order to strengthen their power base.

Bureaucratic organizations can be a driver of corruption also in countries where state structures seem to function fairly well. Consider how the risk of corruption depends on the interaction between civil servants and between a civil servant and clients. If clients have a legitimate right to services, such as access to elementary school or payments from a pension fund, there is usually less flexibility for discretionary strategies. However, if these clients are in some form of queue, the civil servant may profit from letting them pass the line in exchange for a payment. If not controlled, such circumstances leave the civil servant with an opportunity to "capture the whole demand curve"; that is, to set the size of the bribe and the matching beneficial treatment according to how much each client is able and willing to pay. Even when this form of corruption is limited to letting only a few clients pass the line now and then, it may generate significant returns for the civil servant. Depending on how authority is structured, such risks of corruption may be present, for instance, in the award of hospital services, the recruitment of children to a superior school, or the award of licenses necessary for business purposes.[11]

Moreover, the risks are very different in the case of a civil servant who is in a position to select clients/beneficiaries from a set of alternative firms, individuals, or organizations, as opposed to the case where clients are in position to select a civil servant of their choice. In the first case, when a civil servant *can select clients*, the risk of corruption will depend on the degree of discretionary power associated with his or her authority. In public tenders, for instance, the opportunity to demand bribes will be higher the more specialized, complex, or artistic the goods or services procured are. For more standard products and services, the tender criteria are generally much clearer, and it is harder (but not impossible) for the officer to manipulate the process.[12] In addition to the officers' discretionary power, it matters if decisions are made by one officer alone or as part of a group. Even if corruption will typically decrease as the number of informed decision makers rises, there are also circumstances where those involved will find it "safer" to commit such a crime if they are part of a group of allied decision makers. Group corruption requires significant mutual trust and confidentiality and thus, once these conditions are in place, the crime is harder to reveal and combat.[13]

By contrast, where clients are in position to *select their civil servant*, the form of corruption will depend on whether the officers compete or collude. Consider, for example, the cases when citizens or firms can choose which tax office to contact, what control post to pass, what hospital to use, or which port to use for imports of goods. Some form of competition for clients between public offices, or between officers within a public office, will generally reduce the risk of corruption. If an officer demands a bribe, the client can consult a colleague or another office. The situation is quite different, however, if the officers within an institution or across institutions collude, so that a bribe is demanded regardless of who a client addresses. How bureaucratic organizations determine the risk of corruption and how this risk plays out in practice is described by Sequeira and Djankov (2010). Given unique data on corruption in the ports administrations of Durban, South Africa, and Maputo, Mozambique, the authors explain the form of corruption as a function of institutional features. They distinguish between (administrative) *collusive corruption*, when public officials and private agents share the rents generated by corruption, and *coercive corruption*, a less-coordinated form of corruption involving higher or less predictable bribes. Collusive corruption reduces the expenses for the firms involved, while coercive corruption imposes higher costs on firms. In this study, where competition in markets was relatively well secured despite the corruption, the latter form of corruption was found to have the most distortive direct effects in the economy. Firms were found to accept relatively large extra transport expenses to avoid unpredictable demands for bribes. It was also found that corrupt demands were less frequent in services offered by privately owned entities. Instances of corruption were more frequent, however, where the interaction between those involved in port service provision and the firms was higher. In this specific case, the risk of corruption was higher in Maputo, where most procedures were handled face-to-face and where a policy of rotating staff across different ports and terminals was in effect.[14] In Durban, where clearance documentation was processed online, corrupt demands were less frequent, but when they were made, they took a form that is more difficult to control and thus more persistent.

For anticorruption policy work, it is important to understand how institutional organization matters to the risk of corruption. Even if more empirical results are needed for making sound recommendations, it is clear that corruption in many cases can be reduced, not only by promoting greater transparency, exerting tighter control, and imposing and sanctions but also through administrative reorganization. A more demanding scenario for anticorruption efforts is one in which players collude for corrupt access to assets despite such institutional reforms (see box 2.1 for examples). There can be much to gain for those involved, particularly if the crime can go on over time, and researchers and policy makers should be alert for collusive corruption also in societies with otherwise low levels of corruption.

Box 2.1 Collusive Corruption: Not Just a Developing-Country Phenomenon

British Broadcasting Corporation (BBC) News Europe reported on October 4, 2013, that about 50 people, including two former mayors and a city planning chief, were convicted in a huge corruption scandal in the Spanish city of Marbella. Tight relationships between Spanish politicians and the construction sector are discussed by Bel, Estache, and Foucart (2014), who point at political corruption as the main reason for overinvestment and oversupply of infrastructure in the country.

The Elf oil company corruption scandal involved political leaders in France and several African countries (Joly 2007). Oil concessions were secured in exchange for bribes, but the scam included theft and illegitimate allocation of large funds to political and business allies. According to the *Guardian*, Elf became "a private bank for executives who spent £200 million on political favors, mistresses, jewelry, fine art, villas and apartments" (*Guardian*, November 12, 2007).

In Italy, there have been numerous cases where civil servants and politicians have been found guilty in collaborating with the Mafia (Del Monte and Papagni 2007; Vannucci 2009).

box continues next page

Box 2.1 Collusive Corruption: Not Just a Developing-Country Phenomenon *(continued)*

The 'Ndrangheta mafia alone is assumed to have an annual revenue comparable to 3–4 percent of Italy's gross domestic product (GDP). Its crime activities include extortion, prostitution, and illegal trade, but it has been increasingly involved in apparently legal business operations that involve government contracts in several European countries.

Another eye-opener was the British BAE case involving, for several decades, one of the world's biggest weapon producers, BAE Systems, as well as British politicians and government representatives in at least five countries (see the *Guardian's* website under "The BAE files"). The transactions were made via UK-controlled tax havens, and the British government representatives involved and informed about the case knew the dealings were morally and legally wrong. Investigations started in the early 2000s, around the time that the Organisation for Economic Co-operation and Development (OECD) antibribery convention and the United Nations (UN) Convention Against Corruption had been signed (in 1997 and 2000, respectively).

In the United States, there have been several cases of collusive corruption where elected or high-ranking government representatives have secured benefits for allies in the private and public sectors. One of the most several cases involved a number of New York officials who were able to influence real estate and construction projects. Other cases involved Illinois governor Rod Blagojevich and a high-ranking Ohio civil servant, Jimmy Dimora, who was sentenced to 28 years in prison on 33 charges of corruption.

Corporate Structures and Secret Identities

It is also important to understand how players in the private sector can be "organized for corruption." This is obviously true when it comes to how large corporations are organized in a network of smaller entities and shell companies registered in tax havens and secrecy jurisdictions to avoid paying taxes or hide their involvement in criminal activities, such as organized crime, tax evasion, or corruption.[15] Financial centers offer a range of business-facilitating services demanded not only by players with criminal intentions but more frequently by legitimate firms with no intention of operating illegally. Increasingly, small and medium-size firms use these structures to simplify entry into a market or (legally) avoid taxes and the competitive disadvantage of operating with higher costs than other market players. Once they are registered in a financial center, however, various illegal benefits become more accessible, particularly if the center operates as a "secrecy jurisdiction." Structures established to facilitate financial secrecy are *drivers of corruption*. Secret ownership makes it possible for players to profit from a well-functioning, market-based capital system while avoiding the risk of being held responsible when they themselves break the rules.

Over the last five years or so, a number of research reports (more often released by nongovernmental organizations and journalists than by academic institutions) have demonstrated how financial secrecy facilitates crime and tax avoidance.[16] Not only are state revenues stolen and taxes not paid, illegal assets become accessible through manipulation of an international financial system

Drivers of Corruption • http://dx.doi.org/10.1596/978-1-4648-0401-4

consisting of fragmented national rules designed primarily to serve domestic interests, not the international financial system as a whole. The assets appear as if "generated," but indirectly, via various financial and corporate structures, they are stolen from citizens, mortgage holders, shareholders who are not aware of the game, aid recipients, and others. Laws designed to secretly secure large amount of a nation's revenue reduce taxes that would otherwise accrue to other countries. Secrecy jurisdictions seem to ignore the crime-facilitating impacts their laws can have, and act without recognition of the international public good achieved by fair markets and high-functioning taxation. In addition, inadequate international collaboration in coordinating financial controls, cross-country investigations and exchanges of evidence, returns of stolen assets, and reporting standards provides even more space for corruption.[17]

The risk of corruption is also something to be aware of when competitors collaborate in joint ventures, relocate their headquarters, or divide their business into several firms for no clear reasons. They engage in these activities for a number of legitimate purposes, but some firms may be motivated to take advantage of the current patchwork of international anticorruption legislation and enforcement. Players in the same market may face different levels of risk in being detected and sanctioned for participating in corrupt activities, particularly because the risk of being sanctioned at home is not the same in other countries.[18] If bribes are expected to determine contract outcomes, such asymmetries are likely to affect not only contract allocations and terms but also framework conditions and collaboration between firms.[19] A court case involving a US-based firm in Kazakhstan, for example, found the company guilty of paying bribes to civil servants for contracts in the country, including when entering into contracts with a conglomerate consisting of four international oil companies. In this case it is notable that the country's state-owned company, which had no ownership shares in this international conglomerate, was found to have influenced the conglomerate's contract allocations via bribe payments. The four international oil companies in the conglomerate were not accused of corruption.[20]

Uncertain Information about Corruption

Exclusive access to information can be a driver of corruption, even when the information is about corruption itself. Consider the interaction between the market players and the agents and middlemen they use when entering a market. Although firms complain about the risk of being held legally responsible for what their far-away partners and daughter companies might do to secure business, the classic argument that agents are facilitators of firms' involvement in corruption is highly relevant.[21] The more a market is distorted by corruption, and the greater the asymmetry between competitors in terms of the consequences of being caught engaging in corruption, the more valuable is an agent's expertise.

Without generalizing about the many consultants who provide essential business-facilitating services, there are circumstances in which agents can become drivers of corruption. The fact that corruption is a hidden and illegal phenomenon makes the agent's advice particularly important for players with less information than the agent. Even if a firm entering a market has knowledge about the level of corruption—provided, for example, by corruption-perception indices, business surveys, or business-climate consultants—the firm is still not informed about what is required in its unique situation. A poor ranking for a country on a corruption index suggests for the entrant that corruption might become an issue but it is still unclear what other firms will do to obtain contracts and how far operations can proceed without losing contracts to competitors that offer bribes. This uncertainty can be exploited by agents, middlemen, and lawyers who offer advice, especially to newcomers in markets, but also to more established firms that face challenges interacting with government institutions. Although more research is needed to describe how the mechanisms play out in practice, it is known that some facilitating agents and consultants play a central role in corruption; for example, when they are in a position to suggest that a payment would be "wise" simply to secure a "fair process" because other players are likely to be paying bribes.[22] Inasmuch as a firm would naturally prefer as much distance from a bribe payment as possible, an agent's proposal of taking care of bribe transactions (put in less direct wording, of course) is likely to be accepted if bribery is perceived by the firm as necessary. The agent is thus placed in an excellent position to pocket part if not all of the payment, and may find it advantageous to encourage bribery regardless of what other players do, exacerbating corruption-related challenges in doing so.[23] For the agent, who profits from the client's lack of verifiable information, the mechanism functions better as the level of perceived corruption rises, particularly because a firm's aversion to risk could accelerate such a process instead of curbing it.[24]

The practice of using agents who can easily profit from asymmetric information is just one way in which perceptions of corruption can impact actual levels of corruption. As Andvig and Moene (1990) explain, for both the demand and supply sides of bribes, more (perceived) corruption makes it easier to find a corrupt counterpart, including individuals who can help a firm get out of the trouble if caught in a crime. In addition, a higher estimated level of corruption may reduce an individual's moral costs of committing a crime. Research in psychology, including experimental studies, confirms a tendency to "steal more the more others steal."[25] Hence, the estimates of perceived levels of corruption may benefit those who see an interest in driving the real levels of corruption. Perceptions-based corruption indicators motivate governments to engage in anticorruption reform; as a side-effect, they may also induce players to adapt to what they "know" is the level of corruption, sometimes by offering bribes.

Interventions to Fix Market Failure

Competition is a mechanism that improves price-quality combinations for buyers in both public and private sectors while also encouraging innovation and higher productivity. At the same time, competitive pressure prevents firms from generating profit, motivating many firms to create obstacles to competition whenever possible. Some obstacles are patently illegal, such as those created through clear-cut violations of competition laws and principles: for example, cartel collaboration, tender corruption, and payments made to politicians or high-ranking civil servants with sector oversight responsibility (for example, to get unfavorable decisions by the competition/antitrust authorities overruled).[26] Other obstacles maybe the result of legitimate actions, such as lobbying, but they may also be the result of collusive corruption: for example, firms may obtain beneficial treatment in court cases, secure tax deductions or tax breaks, get cheap access to credit and subsidies, overcome trade barriers, influence tender criteria to match their comparative advantages, and seek government influence to win tenders abroad.[27]

Obstacles to competition can be a problem in any market, but in some sectors, such as the natural monopolies, it is especially difficult to make market mechanisms function. In the provision of essential services—such as providing electricity or water and transportation infrastructure—scale effects, investment risks, and political sensitivities are typically present. The results are generally observed in the form of *market failures;* that is, private or state-owned firms functioning inadequately, obtaining exorbitant state subsidies, or generating unacceptably large profits. In these contexts, it is important to be aware that the need for government intervention to fix market failure may itself be a driver of corruption. This is mainly due to the ease with which corruption can be hidden in the management of large (and potentially tempting) assets, such as state-owned entities and the regulation of utility networks. Tenders for public-private partnerships (PPP) can be manipulated without raising suspicion of corruption, and, likewise, state-owned firms can be privatized while their market power remains intact.[28] Even clear-cut corruption can be kept "safely hidden" in complex financing schemes and contracts, which are often kept confidential or difficult for outsiders to control.[29] The expected government intervention (for example, regulation, privatization, and other reforms) creates an arena for political corruption; in exchange for benefits, market failures are allowed to continue. The variety of relevant political concerns and priorities in service delivery (for example, pricing, protecting domestic industry, attracting foreign direct investment, avoiding cream skimming, and protecting the environment) makes it possible for those in charge to defend almost any political decision. The obvious fact that utility regulation is difficult can be the best excuse for suboptimal outcomes.

While such risks are particularly pronounced in utilities, there are similar distortions in other sectors too. Health and education, for example, are sectors with significant state regulation, especially if private providers play a significant role in service provision, and market failure can be a challenge at different stages of the sector value chain. For example, competition is easily impeded in supply markets, such as markets for textbooks or pharmaceutical products, and indicators of leakage of allocated funds, "ghost workers," and other dysfunctions reveal significant weaknesses in service delivery.[30] Another sector exposed to market failure is state-financed construction. Projects are not only complex, expensive, and difficult to control; with a high risk of collusion between competitors, there are, as Wells (2014) explains, fundamental flaws in how the sector is governed. At the planning stage and procurement, the formal procedures are designed as if a larger amount of information is present than what is actually the case. In practice, decision makers do not have a full overview of financial matters, future demand for services and buildings, or technical obstacles, and they frequently have to adjust or deviate from former decisions. The need for addressing new concerns and facts along the way, and sometimes for renegotiating contracts, is a common feature of the sector and rarely questioned from an anticorruption perspective. Under such circumstances, where pragmatic departure from plans and programs is expected, it is obviously easier to facilitate corruption. According to Flyvbjerg, Bruzelius, and Rothengatter (2003), there is also a strong tendency among "all the players around the table" to inflate the size of projects, the total cost, and the demand estimates.[31] Corruption and excess spending are thus consequences of serious dysfunctions in sector governance and organization.

Investigation and prosecution of corruption on a case-by-case basis is always important, but sustainable solutions depend on how well the underlying causes are understood and the ability to detect market and sector distortions as either a consequence or a driver of corruption. Anticorruption should not necessarily include the same "best practice" and "one size fits all" initiatives across sectors. The most exposed sectors especially may require rethinking regarding how they are governed and whether it is possible to promote more robust decision-making processes, given their unique characteristics.

Revenues from the Export of Natural Resources

A further driver of corruption is the access to revenues from abroad. In a study of Iran, Islamic Rep. in the 1950s, Mahdavy (1970) defined the term *external rents* as "rentals paid by foreign individuals, concerns or governments to individuals, concerns or governments of a given country," and *rentier states* as "countries that receive on a regular basis substantial amounts of external rents." External rents are often associated with the revenues from export of nonrenewable resources, for which the world market price is often much higher than what it takes to extract the resources. The term applies also to funds offered in aid or cheap loans, discussed later.

Revenues accrued from the production of nonrenewable resources, such as petroleum and minerals, have the potential to boost an economy, but are also associated with a spiral of events that are damaging to development. Various players may try to get in position to benefit from these revenues, including by help of corruption. Competition for influential positions sharpens. Incumbent politicians find it more important to stay in power and may undermine democratic mechanisms to avoid being replaced by another network of allies (who would then control the revenues).[32] Moreover, revenues from resource production reduce a government's need for tax revenues, thus diminishing "the need" to prove political legitimacy through healthy reinvestment of tax payer money. If democracy is also rendered dysfunctional, incumbents can govern as they like with little risk of being punished by unsatisfied voters.[33] This is particularly so if the military is supportive, and for this reason, military leaders are sometimes paid a share of the revenues, raising the level of malfeasance to what could be called *kleptocratic* corruption (see the glossary in chapter 1). Obviously, such political developments in *rentier states* weaken the general accountability of government to citizens and thus also the quality of state administrative functioning. These developments are typically followed by increased income disparity, further enlarging the distance between citizens and the state, as well as a weakening of the political focus on industrial development in other sectors of the economy.[34] As citizens become more disappointed with the ruling regime, civil society reactions are usually oppressed by the government. These circumstances reflect a negative correlation between revenues from natural resource production and income levels per capita, a phenomenon often referred to as the *resource curse*.[35]

There are many legitimate reasons why development is difficult as a country starts generating revenues from the sales of natural resources, as described by Humphreys, Sachs, and Stiglitz (2007). The gloomy spiral of events described above is not a curse that cannot be prevented, but corruption is clearly among the most serious threats to development in these environments.[36] It is worth noting how the difficulties may begin before any rents have materialized. The sheer expectation of revenues from the industry can lead to higher levels of corruption if various players and stakeholders do whatever they can, legal or not, to get in position for a share of the future revenues. A study by Vicente (2010, 2011) of two islands that are in many ways similar, Cape Verde and São Tomé and Príncipe, reveals how corruption increased in one of the societies when oil was found. The oil revenues never appeared because the resources could not be commercialized, but the expectations of revenues triggered a number of rent-seeking activities and caused an increase in the level of corruption.

Whether and how the challenges arise is context specific, however. As emphasized by Le Billion (2012, 2014), it is important to distinguish between different forms of governance failure that prevent society from gaining from the revenues and developing, and to recognize underlying conflicts and security threats posed by rents from natural-resource production. While corruption at different levels requires different solutions, "everything" should not come under the "corruption" label. Illegal exploitation of resources and tax evasion are different forms of crime, and the beneficiaries are often firms or players abroad. The drivers of corruption vis-à-vis tax evasion and the illegal exploitation of informal exports must be identified at different stages of industry development and production, and matched with who the responsible players are based on understanding. The literature on the resource curse has come a long way in explaining the incentive problems in politics, but it has not delivered many solutions for initiating reform. A main message, however, is that high-functioning political institutions are a precondition for successful sector regulation.[37]

Development Aid and Loans

The money transferred in development aid and cheap loans comes from abroad, usually without any productivity-related efforts from the recipient society, and these funds are at risk of grabbing of the sort associated with revenues from the extractive industries. However, while revenues from extractive industries make the government less dependent on foreign support, development aid by contrast is typically followed by collaboration with recipient governments, demand for institutional performance, more external control and transparency, as well as competence-raising programs. Charron (2011) finds lower levels of perceived corruption associated with collaboration with development partners; for the last two decades, the effect has been stronger with multinational development support than with bilateral support. Given generalized perceptions-based indicators of corruption, it is difficult to draw optimistic conclusions about causality between development support and a reduced level of corruption for a period in which many forms of internal and external anticorruption pressures are present, but at least the study does not support the not uncommon assumption that development aid increases the level of corruption.

One of the particular challenges when offering aid, however, is the "Samaritan's dilemma," which refers to an aid-offering government's altruism. The more urgent the development needs, the more the aid-offering entity pays, and the weaker the recipient government's incentives to perform better, because better performance will eventually cut the level of aid received.[38] The desire to offer financial and other forms of support is particularly strong in emergency situations and in the most-fragile states. Huge amounts of financial development support have been brought into catastrophe areas such as the tsunami-hit areas in Asia, Haiti after the 2010 earthquake, and South Sudan due to the dramatic refugee situation, the lack of infrastructure, and the fact that state-building must start from scratch. Such sets of circumstances are vulnerable to theft and corruption because oversight systems are weak and funds "pour in" from many sources, continuing as long as the needs are dire.

These circumstances suggest a need for separating studies of causality between development partner presence and reduced corruption into several subquestions; the correlation may depend on levels of development and emergency, and be different for different forms of corruption challenges. The Samaritan's dilemma, for example, is likely to distort the positive correlation between aid and/or development loans and reduced corruption in some circumstances, but not for all categories of developing countries. For an incumbent developing-country government in an adequately stable situation, tax revenues that are contingent upon better economic performance offer a more sustainable source of revenue compared to a strategy of "demonstrating poverty." If so, the Samaritan's dilemma and its associated corruption risks are an issue primarily for the weakest aid recipients and emergency situations.

The conditionality associated with aid and lending—"perform or we won't give you more"—seems difficult for donor agencies to keep under any circumstances, however. Foreign development support might become a steady source of benefits for the corrupt, regardless of whether explicit performance targets have been reached. A further difficulty for donors is to balance expectations of institutional accountability with efforts to exercise external control. Comprehensive control may become de facto parallel state functions and undermine the efforts of "using government systems."[39]

There are also drivers of corruption and accessible assets within the development-aid community itself. Many authors have pointed at incentive problems of donor agencies, and there are a number of examples where representatives of donor agencies have been involved in illegal transactions or activities that violate their organization's rules and the recipient country's legislation.[40] Although donor agencies are aware of the potentially troubling impact of such cases on the legitimacy of their operations, they, like other bureaucracies, have encountered difficulties eradicating the challenges completely and handling revealed cases of fraud and corruption effectively. Jansen (2014) describes such weaknesses based on eye-witness experience from Tanzania, where large amounts of Norad-financed support for natural-resource protection disappeared. In Jansen's view, the Norwegian government's reaction was inadequate considering that the case had few, if any, consequences for the bilateral collaboration between the two countries and only a small share of the disappeared funds was returned to Norway. Furthermore, Jansen explains a donor-government's institutional disincentives to react partly as a trade-off between the cost of exercising control and the ease of referring to recipient responsibilities. Among the factors is the low propensity among donor representatives to procure independent reviews and audits of aid-financed projects and programs. Sometimes these are driven by the need to seize opportunities for new projects, without giving much attention to the performance of projects already started or making retrospective assessments of what did or did not work. According to Jansen, this tendency is intensified by heavy workloads and "pipeline problems"; that is, when funds have to be allocated within the timeframe of a financial year regardless of the status of preparatory work or controls. The faith in "best practice" solutions might have overshadowed the need for contextual understanding and process evaluation, and when it comes to anticorruption specifically, he describes a "futuristic attitude"—instead of addressing (sensitive) cases in the past, the preference is for supporting new anticorruption institutions and training programs. The general norm-generating value of holding those involved responsible has not gained much ground in development-financed anticorruption policy work.

It remains unclear whether weak incentives to react to revealed cases of corruption and fraud in recipient state administrations and organizations are to be explained by subtle benefits of not reacting and/or costs associated with the act of reacting. Despite ample anecdotal evidence in donor communities, there is limited systematically collected evidence to confirm the listed factors. Despite unclear conclusions regarding development-partner internal-incentive problems and recipient-country weaknesses, there are good reasons to be aware of how aid and cheap loans can drive corruption in developing countries: There will be members of the recipient community who are prone to spend time and effort in getting into a position of power that will allow them to benefit from such funds while controls are still generally weak in developing countries. The difficulty of letting development aid and cheap loans be followed by efficient anticorruption strategies is not just a matter of recipient-state administration, however; it must also be understood in light of government priorities within the high-income donor countries.

Notes

1. The effort of securing extra assets is often described in the literature as *rent-seeking*, which refers to the investment of time and money to secure assets and benefits for oneself in ways that are not directly rewarding for society at large; that is, they are unproductive activities. The *rents* in rent-seeking are excess values obtained when the returns of an investment are higher than the net balance. Primary literature on rent seeking includes Krueger (1974), Rose-Ackerman (1978), Buchanan, Tollison, and Tullock (1980), Tollison (1982), and Bhagwati (1982). See Lambsdorff (2002b), and Harstad and Svensson (2011) for distinctions between corruption and rent-seeking.

2. For early analyses of the risk of corruption as a function of institutional organization, see Rose-Ackerman (1978), Tirole (1986), and Shleifer and Vishny (1993). For recent use of industrial organization theory to understand corruption in the private sector, see Celentani and Ganuza (2002), Fisman and Svensson (2007), Søreide (2008), and Lambert-Mogliansky (2011).

3. See Raballand and Marteu (2014), Musila and Sigué (2010), and Sequeira and Djankov (2010).

4. Challenges described by Bertrand et al. (2007), who studied driving schools in India. Not only would candidates bribe to obtain a driving license without the required qualifications; candidates with sufficient competence to pass were denied their driving license if negating corruption.

5. For a discussion of corruption in education, see Poisson (2014) and UNDP (2011).

6. One civil servant alone may not be able to create the "needed" shortage. Group involvement will be addressed below. Corrupt strategies in public procurement are described by Della Porta and Vannucci (1999), Rose-Ackerman (1978, 1999), Moody-Stuart (1997), Piga (2011), and Lambert-Mogliansky (2011), among others.

7. Skaperdas (2001) describes the problem of crime facilitators within crime control units, a problem that has seriously challenged the fight against organized crime, for example in Mexico (well covered by the press).

8. See AIV (2013), a report for the government in The Netherlands on crime, corruption, and instability.

9. By approaching a large number of financial service providers in 182 countries, Findley, Nielson, and Sharman (2012) estimated how easy it is to organize and hide corruption, terrorist financing, and tax evasion by help of secrecy jurisdictions (tax havens).

10. Susan Rose-Ackerman (1999, 2010a) explains how shortage, theft, and extortion determine the consequences of the corruption for society.

11. For relevant analyses, see Lui (1985) and Rose-Ackerman (1978).

12. For nuances on tender-related corruption, see references in the "Shortage and Illegality" section (misuse of authority) and the "Revenues from the Export of Natural Resources" section.

13. Gong (2002) provides examples of network corruption in China; the biggest case, from Zhanjiang, included more than 100 civil servants across institutions, many of them top-level officials.

14. Rotation of civil servants is sometimes used as an anticorruption strategy but may work counterintuitively if, for instance, civil servants "use the opportunity while in a given office," as found by Andvig and Barasa (2014) in a study of police corruption in Kenya. By contrast, in his experimental studies of corruption, Abbink (2004) found staff rotation to cause a sharp decrease in the size of bribes and incidents of corruption, a result explained by lower mutual trust among the players involved.

15. For details of how secrecy jurisdictions are used to cover corruption, see the World Bank Grand Corruption Cases Database Project and the "Puppet Masters" report (De Willebois et al. 2011), which reveal the use of shell companies in large corruption cases. http://www.star.worldbank.org.

16. See the various chapters in Reuter (2012), Norwegian Official Reports (2009), Global Witness (2009), Shaxson (2011), Reed and Fontana (2011), Sharman (2010, 2012) and various reports by Publish What You Pay, http://www.publishwhatyoupay.org/en/resources, the Tax Justice Network, and Global Financial Integrity (http://www.gfintegrity.org/).

17. Tax Justice Network publishes an annual Financial Secrecy Index, http://www.financialsecrecyindex.com/. See Bracking (2012), Christensen (2012), Shaxson (2011), and Ndikumana and Boyce (2011). The report returns to this theme when discussing policy challenges in chapter 4.

18. See the OECD website for country reports on the implementation of the OECD Anti-Bribery Convention. Results are summarized by Transparency International (2012).

19. Bjorvatn and Søreide (2013) study how asymmetric risk of sanctions distorts contract outcomes. They find that asymmetry increases bribe-averse firms' incentives to offer bribes, but there are also instances where competition between good solutions and bribes improved the bribe-averse firms' price-quality offer. See also Engel, Goerg, and Yu (2012) for discussion.

20. Securities and Exchange Commission: Litigation Release No. 20094/April 26, 2007 and Accounting and Auditing Enforcement Release No. 2602/April 26, 2007. See also the client memorandum by Willkie Farr & Gallagher LLP.

21. Using a theoretical model, Hasker and Okten (2008) explain how key anticorruption policy mechanisms can be rendered dysfunctional by the use of intermediaries, how such agents enhance the distortive effects of corruption, and why these games must be understood to fight business corruption. See also Bray (2005) and Moody-Stuart (1997) for discussion of how some middlemen drive corruption.

22. Using these suggested mechanisms, Drugov, Hamman, and Serra (2011) consistently find the presence of intermediaries to facilitate and increase levels of corruption when tested in experiments.

23. See Hasker and Okten (2008), Lambsdorff (2002a), and chapter 10 in Rose-Ackerman (1978) for relevant nuances.

24. Søreide (2009) finds risk-averse players to be more inclined to offer bribes if the level of corruption is high, because the higher the level of corruption, the higher the risk of failing with an honest business approach.

25. For results, see Falk and Fishbacher (2002), Goette, Huffman, and Meyer (2006), and Dŭsek, Ortmann, and Lizal (2005). Bobkova and Egbert (2012) provide a review.

26. Laffont (2005) offers a useful analysis of competition and implications for regulation under weak institutional framework conditions. For further discussion, see Estache and Wren-Lewis (2009), Søreide (2012), and Benitez, Estache, and Søreide (2012).

27. The forms of influence can take legal forms while still implying exchange of "close to corrupt"-benefits, including campaign funding, revolving-door positions, generously rewarded board membership, and more. See Mueller (2003) and Drazen (2000) for comprehensive reviews of relevant public-choice literature. Grossman and Helpman (2001) and Ackerman and Ayres (2004) analyze mechanisms associated with special-interest influence on politics.

28. For discussion of PPPs and corruption-related challenges, see Estache and Philippe (2012), Sanghi, Hankinson, and Sundakov (2007), and Akerele and Gidado (2003). Guasch (2004) describes how easily such contractual terms are renegotiated as part of corrupt or "half-corrupt" schemes. When it comes to privatization, selling with market power means not only a higher acquisition price for the government (often highly welcomed state revenues), but also an opportunity to secure higher bribes. See Ades and Di Tella (1999), Bjorvatn and Søreide (2005), and Auriol and Straub (2011) for relevant analyses. For reviews of empirical evidence, see Manzetti (1999) on cases from Latin America; and Puntillo (1996) and Black, Kraakman, and Tarassova (2000) on cases from the Russian Federation.

29. The problem might be worse in countries with weak institutions, but this is also a serious issue in OECD countries. See Estache (2011), a volume on challenges in utility regulation in Europe.

30. Poisson (2014) describes different forms of corruption-related practices in the education sector, with examples from three countries. See also UNDP (2011). For cases of leakage in education, see Oubda (2013), Reinikka and Svensson (2004), and Chua (1999). On corruption in health, see, for instance, Falkingham (2004), Vian, Gryboski, Sinoimeric and Hall (2006), and Lindkvist (2012). Hussmann and Rivillas (2014) describe corruption in the funding of pharmaceuticals in Colombia.

31. See also Flyvbjerg and Molloy (2011), Stansbury (2005), Kenny (2009), and De Valence (2011).

32. Mechanisms are explained by Robinson, Torvik, and Verdier (2006) and Torvik (2009).

33. See Brautigam, Moore, and Fjeldstad (2008) for analytic discussion of the role of the tax system in building and securing state legitimacy and examples of the mentioned mechanisms.

34. Kolstad and Wiig (2012), Hodler (2009), and Page (2008) discuss why rents from natural resources may "crowd out" the political support for industrial development in other sectors. This is an area in need of more research.

35. There is much literature on the negative relationship between development and revenue from the export of nonrenewable natural resources. For reviews of the literature, see Barma et al. (2011), Frankel (2010), Kolstad and Søreide (2009), and Humphreys, Sachs, and Stiglitz (2007) among others.

36. Based on data on corruption in Chinese regions, Dong and Torgler (2012) find corruption to be more widespread in regions with abundant natural resources.

37. See Collier, Van der Ploeg, Spence, and Venables (2009) for suggested approaches. Although aid-financed support for new oil-producing countries used to support primarily institutions for oil regulation, more attention is now directed toward political checks and balances. See Kolstad, Wiig, and Williams (2009) for a discussion of aid for petroleum regulation, and Scanteam (2013) for an evaluation of the Norwegian Oil for Development program.

38. Svensson (2000a, 2000b) explains the challenge of offering aid and how difficult it is to make conditionality work (that is, the Samaritan problem). Knack (2001) takes stock of several aid-related challenges, arguments that led to changes in aid-related policy work in the early 2000s. See also Knack and Rahman (2007) for a study of how aid and development loans may have caused higher levels of corruption. Morrison (2012) explains why incentive problems associated with aid and cheap loans prevent successful support of developing countries by avoiding the resource curse. Under some circumstances, he argues, OECD countries should not buy the resources exported.

39. Using government systems for control of spending is one of the principles listed in the Paris Declaration and Accra Agenda for Action. This declaration was never meant to give donor agencies an excuse for skipping the effort of needed controls; it was meant to promote stronger institutions nationally. Support from donor agencies and collaboration are often welcomed in developing countries; for example by audit institutions. See Søreide, Tostensen, and Skage (2012) for a field study where the need for such audit competence-raising initiatives was requested by leaders of such institutions (this is an area with potentially significant anticorruption impacts). Development partners' success in controlling outcomes of competence-raising programs was mixed.

40. At the World Bank, for example, such challenges, as described by Mallaby (2004) and analyzed by authors in Pincus and Winters (2003), led to significant reforms, with the purpose of raising integrity levels through ethical training, added controls, and clearer lines of responsibility.

CHAPTER 3

Exploiting Opportunities and Condoning the Practice

Although the listed sources of rents and assets may offer opportunities for grabbing and clear-cut corruption, these opportunities are not necessarily exploited. Compromised integrity and various risks entail trade-offs for those involved.

This section addresses the question of why some individuals take advantage of opportunities for corruption while others stay honest. Recent psychological insights have brought further understanding, yet it is hard to ascribe certain human traits as "particularly corrupt." Moreover, for pervasive corruption to continue over time, it has to remain undiscovered or condoned, while counter-reactions to the crime stay weak or nonexistent. What is needed to explain corruption is not only an understanding of the different contexts and the propensities of those involved but also an answer to the question of why individuals and institutions that are supposed to prevent and fight corruption remain passive. Several branches of the literature contribute explanatory factors. This brief review lists incentive problems involving staff and management within organizations, the role of individual whistle-blowers, and the responsibilities of firms and organizations that are tasked with observing and acting on cases of corruption among market players. Will they react against it or profit from adapting to it? The ultimate deceit is often associated with elected politicians who take bribes or condone corruption, a challenge addressed in the last part of the section. As will be seen, persistent corruption is a matter of human behavior and social motivation, but state structures and the functions of markets matter as well.

The Individual Decision Maker

The prospect of self-enrichment is a strong motivating force for most people. Self-survival and the competition for resources have shaped human nature and, undeniably, the inclination to secure benefits for oneself and one's clan is still a basic human trait. In fact, since natural selection would be expected to favor selfishness, including dishonesty and illegal acts such as theft and corruption, it is, from the perspective of evolutionary psychology, rather the evolution of *selfless* behavior that is difficult to explain. However, most societies seem to have reached an equilibrium where the mutual benefits obtained by trading favors with other members of a society, including recognition of ownership and other rights, are acknowledged. Usually, such equilibrium also implies recognition of state structures as a way of facilitating framework conditions for survival, production, and reproduction; therefore, acts of corruption among those who are trusted to make decisions on behalf of the many are rarely accepted.[1]

This evolutionary perspective on individual motivations is consistent with theories that explain corruption as the result of rational choice. The theory of individual *utility maximization* postulates quite simply that an individual will be involved in corruption if the benefits associated with the act are expected to outweigh the costs.[2] The relevant literature describes relevant factors in the equation; that is, those factors that constitute costs and benefits in the mind of the individual. The expected benefits obviously include monetary gains as well as positions and power for oneself, one's family, or one's allies. The list of possible costs consists of the bribe payment, moral "costs" of violating norms and rules, efforts to hide the crime and money laundering, as well as the perceived risk of detection and the consequences of prosecution and punishment. Indirect consequences could be the reputational cost if the corruption is revealed, including a loss of status and future income, for example, as the result of debarment from work positions or tenders. In some situations, such indirect costs exceed the direct consequence of a sentence.[3]

The utility maximization concept (that is, the trade-off between benefits and costs) is based on assumptions of rational and informed players who know their own preferences and are able to predict and rank the likely outcomes of alternative choices. Even if such assumptions may seem naïve, given our many intellectual shortcomings, the concept is far more useful than theories that otherwise assume more-random decision making or decisions steered by framework conditions. Moreover, it matches the fundamental role of the rationality assumption in criminal justice systems. Placing blame and sentencing would make no sense if individuals were not assumed to steer their own decisions, and some degree of conscious goal targeting must be assumed if preventive impacts are expected. Whether and to what extent this assumption holds true is nevertheless much debated and represents an important question in any efforts to understand crime (and its drivers) and the effect of law enforcement initiatives.[4] Although the answer depends on individuals, contexts, and forms of crime, one can reasonably assume that corruption is a result of fairly rational decision making, and more so than many other forms of crime. Most of the literature assumes that corruption is more or less the result of strategic planning by highly competent and informed players who are representatives of firms and government institutions and who are able to assess the probability of the various outcomes of their crime.

Law Enforcement and Sanctions

If the propensity to be involved in corruption depends on rational assessment of benefits and costs, an individual will be less likely to exploit opportunities for corruption if the costs associated with the crime increase.[5] There is significant variation across countries in how severely corruption is punished. In some countries, detention is rarely used as a punishment, or the number of years in prison is very low, while in others, punishment may exceed 20 years of imprisonment. Nevertheless, these variations hardly explain the variations in the level of crime. For example, some countries with low repression levels, such as the Nordic countries, are perceived as significantly less corrupt than most countries with more draconian penalties. Moreover, the deterrent effect of heavier penalties is uncertain and modest at best. This elasticity[6] varies across forms of crime, but even if the strength of the correlation grows with the level of rationality of the criminal, other factors might be far more decisive for propensity to be involved.

In addition to deal- and context-specific factors, the risk of being detected seems far more important than the length of a custodial sentence; therefore, it is significantly more effective to increase investigation efforts, and thus the potential offender's perceived risk of being caught in the crime, than to increase the number of years the offender is kept imprisoned.[7] Hence, the economic literature, which has traditionally postulated a clear connection between (more) severe penalties and lower levels of crime, is now starting to modify some of these assumptions. Being found guilty implies an enormous individual cost that increases in proportion to the eradication of one's image of being a reliable and successful member of society. Nevertheless, the process of being investigated, accused, and brought to court is generally ignored by many authors. This is especially true when it comes to economists who provide some of the most solid statistical analyses of the relationship but tend to count the number of years in prison and the size of the fine as the main indicators in their analysis of the deterrent effect of a criminal justice system. The importance of *placing blame* is largely left out of law and economic models, regardless of its core purpose in the criminal justice system and its potentially moderating impact on postulated "need" for (costly) years in prison. Overlooking the costs associated with criminal law process may have led to some erroneous conclusions.

Although increasing the risk of detection and reacting against guilty individuals are effective anticorruption criminal law approaches, they are not always possible or practical.[8] In cases of corruption, reaction against firms (as "guilty organizations") is an important pragmatic approach to avoiding scapegoats. If criminal justice systems address individual responsibility only, a firm's management and owners can (more) easily point at the individuals involved, let them face the consequences, and continue to make money as usual, whatever the means. There can be cases where it is known that a company has been involved in corruption, and profited from it, but the decision makers cannot be identified. For these reasons, it is also necessary to have the option of sanctioning organizations by criminal or administrative law, even if the individuals involved should be held responsible when possible.[9] Many authors now debate how best to fine-tune corporate sanctions, and not just punish but also incentivize corporate performance consistent with goals for society at large. Arlen (2011, 2012) explains how sanctions can be designed to increase a firm's propensity to inform authorities of crime detected in its organization and collaborate with investigators, while Oded (2011) presents a sanction principle for self-policing rewards. Plea bargaining is another tool available for incentivizing performance, but as clarified by Garoupa and Stephen (2006, 2008), the effect depends very much on how the rules are set and function in practice.

In addition to formal sanctions and penalties, firms and individuals found guilty of corruption can be debarred from taking part in tenders. From a legal perspective, this is not meant to be a punishment for the committed crime; instead, it is an administrative *consequence* of reduced confidence in the given player. The official justification is usually the importance of securing stakeholders' trust in the given procuring agency. In economic terms, however, debarment is considered a contributing factor to the set of costs and risks facing a firm involved in corruption. If lack of trust is what justifies debarment, however, it is difficult to keep a company debarred if it has significantly improved its compliance system and done what it can to become a trustworthy actor.[10] This is why there are debates in many countries about how a formal system of "self-cleaning" should be designed and also why the World Bank offers firms found guilty in corruption to collaborate with investigators and compliance officers on a track to regain the opportunity to bid for World Bank financed contracts.[11] This is a subject for which drawing conclusions about optimal solutions still remains difficult.

Rational in Theory, Irrational in Practice

If the rationality assumption holds, corruption can be predicted quite well by theoretical models, particularly if the theory's underlying assumptions about what matters to a potentially corrupt decision maker match reality. Existing research on corruption, provides useful results explaining how various compensation schemes matter to an individual's inclination to solicit bribes,[12] whether market position matters to such inclinations, when corruption determines the outcome of tenders,[13] how corruption requires mutual trust between those involved,[14] the importance of reward structures and the choice between rent-seeking and productive jobs,[15] a company's choice between campaign finance and corruption when seeking to influence politicians,[16] and how perceived levels of corruption influence the propensity to offer bribes,[17] among topics. How far can such theoretical predictions about individual decision making be trusted? Empirical insights, obtained through interviews, business surveys, and court cases, for example, help get somewhat closer to a good understanding of corrupt behaviors.[18] However, the models' power to explain patterns of corruption will always be obstructed by variation in individuals' perceptions of costs and benefits associated with participating in (or condoning) corruption, as well as varying levels of rationality; everyone makes decisions that deviate from the expected and the rational.

What is remarkable—and to the benefit of those who develop such theories—is that recent behavioral research has found that many irrationalities follow a pattern. This means that theories explaining the incentives to take part in corruption can be adjusted based on decision-making processes, which tend to be systematically irrational, and the validity of which can be quite high despite natural intellectual shortages.[19] For example, it has been found that humans have a strong tendency to prefer rewards today instead of tomorrow (that is, they have a high discount factor). The further away a sentence may be, the less threatening it is and the less likely to influence decisions. Moreover, the perceived risks associated with crime are not linear in the actual probabilities of being detected and prosecuted. Humans are irrationally concerned about big losses and tend to overestimate very small probabilities.[20] At the same time, they tend to underestimate high probabilities and are, in many settings, less concerned about harmful consequences than what the true likelihoods should imply. Yet, women are more risk averse than men.[21] Based on experimental research on corruption, Djawadi and Fahr (2013) have studied the difference between attitude toward risk and individuals' misperception of risk in corrupt decision making. They find miscalculation of risk to be a far more important determinant of corruption than risk attractiveness; the two are very different facets of decision making. Furthermore, the misperception of risk was found to increase in the frequency of an individual's involvement in corrupt acts, which suggests that the preventive impact of detection and sanctions diminish as individuals commit more crimes.

Rationalizing Corruption

One of the human traits better understood now is how one's moral map tends to get blurred when access to large benefits is possible. What behavioral studies also show is that humans are extremely good at rationalizing the unethical if they benefit significantly from the unethical acts. Those involved in corruption will often be able to convince themselves that the crime was "the only right thing to do." A business leader who pays bribes to win contracts may find the crime defensible given the consequences of losing the tender, which could imply a loss of profit and, possibly, dismissal of staff. The broader moral perspectives and personal costs of being caught in corruption would be easily forgotten if some higher end is perceived to justify the crime.[22]

An individual's assessment of the benefits and the costs of being involved in corruption (that is, the decision-making process behind the crime) will be affected by "how well" he or she is able to rationalize the crime.[23] Such rationalization crowds out feelings of guilt and shame that could otherwise have prevented an individual from committing the crime. Although this inclination to rationalize crime may depend on a number of factors, what an individual has (or has not) been taught about honest and ethical values, as well as the influence and attitudes of colleagues, seems to matter decisively.[24] Even individuals with "mature moral perspectives" are likely to be influenced by their work environment.

Institutions respond to basic psychological needs, and for this reason individuals are prone to adapt to, rather than deviate from, their cultures. By help of economic analysis, Tirole (1996) explains why newcomers in a company are likely to adopt the work ethics of their colleagues, discussing why this is relevant to understanding variation in organizations' propensity to be involved in corruption.

Another important factor in the individual's attempt to rationalize corruption is the physical or cultural distance to the victims of the crime, typically the members of the society where the corruption takes place. The more an individual embraces a "we/they perspective" on society, the easier it is for him or her to rationalize the crime.[25] Moreover, an individual's feeling of shame and guilt depends on how society responds to the specific form of crime. While some forms of crime, such as murder, discrimination, or violence against children, would normally enrage the population, financial crime is often too complex, distant, or invisible to generate such effects. Even if there are victims when a billion dollars disappear from state assets, it is often difficult to tell exactly who they are and to imagine their faces. According to Van Winden and Ash (2009, 14), "white collar crimes are the product of a technological environment that did not have an analogue in our evolutionary past, and therefore the penetration of these crimes does not present a social stimulus that would easily elicit our anti-free-rider psychological device." Even if there are clear protests against corruption in many countries, this is probably among the forms of crime less likely to elicit such "anti-free-rider devices." If not sufficiently condemned by society, it is less likely to create the feeling of shame and guilt that could otherwise have prevented an individual from committing the crime.

"Society's general opinion" (that is, the common view in society) is thus a factor in understanding the extent of corruption. This opinion will obviously depend on contextual factors. Lack of state legitimacy or low wages, for example, may explain a general tolerance of corruption. Bribes paid or demanded for the delivery of basic services are more likely to be found acceptable in a situation where the provision of public services has broken down. If state authority and structures are systematically misused for corrupt benefits, the general public may find it just as reasonable to adapt pragmatically to the circumstances, even if that implies the payment of bribes.[26] The less trust put in public institutions, the more important informal ties to state officials who control resources and important choices become, and thus, unbiased best practice decision making is hard to put into practice. Furthermore, patronage and ethnicity explain why some civil servants are more loyal to their clan than the institution they represent.[27] It can be striking how an individual's loyalty, feeling of guilt and shame, and moral assessments can turn completely in the opposite direction of values reflected in the (formal) legal framework. From a legal perspective, these explanatory factors are drivers of corruption, while at the same time they reflect fundamental challenges in terms of how norms are developed, how the state functions, and how far the government and its laws are acknowledged by the citizens.

Absence of Reaction in Organizations

Assuming that individuals have a natural tendency to grab (as discussed in the "Individual Decision Maker" section), the sheer absence or failure of structures that are supposed to hinder the illegal and unfair allocation of benefits is itself a driver of corruption because it becomes easier to grab corrupt rents without consequences. The international financial crisis that started in 2008 triggered debates about regulatory failure in the control of financial markets. Research reveals that the institutions established to control and react are not necessarily the ones that report cases and bring them to court. According to Dyck, Morse, and Zingalese (2010), who studied the 216 largest corporate fraud cases in the United States between 1996 and 2004, relatively few cases were revealed by auditors (10 percent of cases), securities regulators (7 percent), or in private litigation (3 percent). Far more important were the reactions by individuals with no explicit role in the corporate governance arena, such as employees (17 percent of cases), nonfinancial market regulators (13 percent), and the media (13 percent). These findings suggest a potential for improving some regulatory institutions and the function of audit services. Equally importantly, they underscore the role of ordinary citizens in the fight against corruption. A reaction from those with first-hand access to information is essential to control corruption, and they are often colleagues or clients of those who benefit from the crime.

Such reaction requires that those individuals who have incentives to react are informed about the crime and, conversely, that those with information about the acts also have incentives to react. Consider the case of a bureaucracy where civil servants act on behalf of their institution and where some of them take bribes. What makes witnesses condone the crime instead of reacting against it? When will staff and manager be motivated by performance and integrity, instead of corruption? In bureaucratic organizations, managers are unable to (and should not be able to) control each and every decision made by their staff. This lack of control is often referred to as a principal-agent problem of asymmetric information, where the *principal* is a benevolent manager or external control body with honest intentions to make sure that the given institution performs well, while *agent* refers to an individual who represents the institution and make choices on its behalf, often outside the principal's (complete) control.[28] Obviously, an agent can exploit the principal's lack of information about how he or she performs, which means that a principal will not know which staff member can be trusted. According to this theory, however, the principal can promote integrity and productivity by making clever choices regarding bureaucratic organization (as discussed in chapter 2), wages, allocation of authority, and monitoring. More specifically, a manager should concentrate monitoring efforts on observable performance and apply some form of incentive contracts for what is less observable. If *decision making* processes are hard to observe (for example, how police officers interact with citizens), there should be more control on outcomes (that is, how well crime is controlled). If *outcomes* are hard to observe (for example, the performance of secret security forces), there should be more control on procedures

Drivers of Corruption • http://dx.doi.org/10.1596/978-1-4648-0401-4

(for example, procedures regarding budget, recruitment, and approval for operations). Incentive contracts include standard performance-based payment schemes
where staff is paid according to their level of performance. Such schemes can
reward honesty and productive work and make it more costly to lose the job if
caught in corruption.

In practice, however, it is difficult for a manager to tailor wages, bonuses, and
sanctions in order to promote integrity.[29] Wages are generally more rigid than
what the theory assumes and cannot necessarily be raised for anticorruption
purposes. Even if they could, the approach would be expensive and, possibly,
unreliable.[30] When it comes to exercising control and reacting to failure, labor
laws generally govern the employee-employer relationship, and it may not be
possible for an employer to introduce sanctions as part of an incentive scheme.
Moreover, in the last decade, research on work compensation has added nuance
to what determines work motivation.[31] Productivity will not necessarily increase
the more it is rewarded, and many performance-based compensation schemes
have failed to deliver expected results.[32] There are different explanations in the
literature. Weibel, Rost, and Osterloch (2010) distinguish between the *standard
economic* management view and the *psychological* view. The former view largely
assumes that individuals react to external incentives in a predictable manner. The
main question under the standard economic management view is how to measure performance, and design and implement a good scheme. The latter view
criticizes performance-based schemes altogether for being based on stimulus-
response assumptions that are too simplistic. These views are not necessarily as
far apart as they may seem. There is now broad consensus that outcome-based
initiatives targeted at civil servants' *extrinsic* motivation should ideally be combined with initiatives that increase their *intrinsic* motivation as well. Intrinsic
motivation, in turn, depends on how civil servants identify with their institution,
expected responsibilities, and experience fair treatment. Otherwise, the net
effect of a performance payment scheme can easily be counterintuitive.
According to Weiebel, Rost, and Ostreloch (2009, 388), "[g]iving someone a
performance-contingent monetary incentive to do something they already enjoy
can decrease his/her motivation to do it as the person is then likely to view its
action as externally driven rather than internally appealing."[33] Moreover, there is
broad consensus that compensation linked to performance increases productivity
primarily when it comes to repetitive work, while the contrary might be true for
work that requires more creative thinking.[34]

What motivates employees is obviously important in anticorruption, because
the willingness to perform well and make an institution function is the opposite
of corruption. So far, anticorruption initiatives have rarely been linked to development outcomes (such as better public-sector service provision) and they are
often process focused (that is, procurement procedures, audit controls, and documents are made available and so on), thus potentially causing suspicion instead
of stimulating integrity. At the same time, it is not easy to motivate intrinsically
and signal expected accountability where more anticorruption control is clearly
warranted.[35] Even if anticorruption efforts can be better informed by a better

understanding of how motivation, compensation, organization, and allocation of responsibility for (honest) service delivery work, more research is needed before a complete set of policy solutions can be put forward.

Condoned by Management

What can be realized when conducting qualitative studies of corruption in a given sector or institution is that managers are sometimes well aware of the challenges and have chosen not to intervene. Obviously, there are examples where the managers themselves are the most corrupt, or agents further down in the hierarchy share the returns with their executives.[36] However, there are also cases where managers condone the practice without gaining from it personally, and this might be surprising because one would expect most honest managers to at least try to make their institution perform well. One intention an otherwise honest manager might have for condoning corruption is to keep staff productive. Some extra benefits for them, legal or not, may be considered acceptable if those benefits make the staff perform well. In other settings, informal payments are considered a device for minimizing the gap between private and public sector remuneration.[37] A study of mismanagement of travel compensation systems in three African countries found that some managers would offer an entire department a few days of per diem travel compensation simply to offer something extra as a reward, even if no trips had been made.[38] Such informal bonuses can also be a way of generating loyalty within the organization. If not personally involved in the staff's corrupt behavior, managers (and/or the firm) might be involved in other forms of offences or failures and may wish to pay for staff's silence. A further explanation for condoning corruption could be a sense of resignation if, for example, the general trust in governance institutions is low. If no one at the political level seems to notice and appreciate good performance, managers may condone staff's illegal practices, rather than try to clean up the system. Such circumstances easily lead to a comprehensive *collective action problem*, a bad equilibrium where most players and stakeholders do not react to corruption or fraud simply because nobody else has an incentive to do so.[39] Being the only one to react becomes too costly and is unlikely to make a difference.

Management's inclination to condone corruption can also be explained by loyalty to nonstate institutions. A manager with staff consisting primarily of members of his or her ethnic group or tribe may want to let "his people" generate as much extra revenue as possible for their families, if that is considered more important than public service delivery for a society consisting of many different ethnic groups. This is clearly an expression of weak state legitimacy, which may be determined by state structures that represent the legacy of an oppressive colonial regime or that are connected to the presence of multiple ethnicities and lack of group identity.[40] Absence of reaction can sometimes be better understood based on the country's history, development, and democratic culture; political scientists point at the need to understand corruption in light of what is associated with *neopatrimonial* states. According to Clapham (1985), this term refers to how informal power structures can pervade political and administrative systems. Civil servants are perhaps accountable to rulers other than those appointed by the formal state administrative system. When the line between private and public spheres is blurred, civil servants and politicians are inclined to use their position for personal gains, and do not necessarily consider it wrong to do so.

Cultural factors are also relevant to understanding variation in individual attitudes to corruption, whether at the managerial or the staff level. Behavioral experiments conducted in Australia, India, Indonesia, and Singapore by Cameron et al. (2009) found significant cross-country differences in attitudes toward corruption. Surprisingly, participants from highly corrupt environments were not found to be the most tolerant to such crime. In another study of culture and corruption, Alatas et al. (2009a) found that foreign students in the United Kingdom tend to retain their home-country corruption norms in the first years of their studies, and then adopt common UK attitudes to corruption as their studies progress. Apparently, the propensity to condone corrupt practice depends on societal factors, and more experience with corruption does not equate to more tolerance to such crime.

The Role of Whistleblowers

Cases of corruption often involve managers, owners, control institutions, higher-ranking civil servants, and politicians who benefit personally from the crime. Employees, colleagues, or clients may be aware of this fact. These witnesses may fear that reacting to the ongoing corruption will involve some form of confrontation, but they may also be reluctant to remain passive because doing so conflicts with their ethical norms. What determines their readiness to speak out or to remain silent? In line with the utility maximizing concept (described in the "Individual Decision Maker" section), the choice depends on a trade-off between values associated with a reaction and the potential risks. The possible gains from reacting include the intrinsic feeling of acting in accordance with integrity values and in anticipation of positive management reactions, such as a career boost or some form of reward. However, these encouraging outcomes may not necessarily materialize, and if they do, it is far from likely that they will exceed the costs of making a reaction. These costs, however, may include the time and effort to document the facts, the risks of getting into a situation where the evidence is found insufficient, and the possible burden of reacting against a colleague. Even in functioning societies, where corruption is rare, witnesses may choose to remain passive because of the risks associated with a reaction. According to Dyck, Morse, and Zingales (2010), a large majority of those who reported a crime in their own firms would not have done so if they had known the associated costs.[41] In countries where crime rates are high, human rights frequently violated, and government corruption widespread, a reaction could result in a fabricated criminal prosecution, in homicide,[42] or, less dramatically, in a cut in funding or authority for the institution that one represents.[43]

Over the last decade or so, there has been an increasing awareness of the individual's difficulty in speaking out about a crime observed. To incentivize individuals to come forward with information about possible misconduct, many governments and organizations have introduced legislation and policies to encourage and protect whistle-blowers. As part of their compliance programs, firms generally encourage staff to report internally any illegal and/or harmful acts, and some programs also call for any names of contacts outside the company. Moreover, some governments offer rewards to individuals who report their firm's involvement in criminal activities; an example is the whistle-blower provision in the US Dodd-Frank Act.[44] In the United States, rewards for speaking out may reach millions of dollars (several cases have exceeded US$30 million). Many practitioners consider such reward mechanisms essential to reveal crimes, a view supported by evidence showing that monetary rewards tend to have an impact on the employee's propensity to speak out.[45] The interesting question for many researchers is whether the rewards are too high or if there are any indirect or counterintuitive impacts of such programs.[46] More specifically, some authors warn about the possible (indirect) risks of *crowding out* intrinsic instincts of responsibility. According to Feldman and Lobel (2009, 40), "where people tend to portray themselves as internally motivated, duty-bound citizens, the reporting decisions of others are instead viewed as opportunistic actions that are primarily driven by external rewards." In other words, if the social stigma attached to reporting is strong, the reward mechanism may lead to less, rather than more, reporting of illegality.

A further concern is how reward programs may undermine compliance systems, as discussed by Blount and Markel (2012). There could be a risk where colleagues or clients who could stop a crime, instead stay silent and collect a reward once the crime has been committed. Moreover, while firms invest much time and money in the implementation of compliance programs, the government-offered bounty encourages employees to go behind those systems and report even before the company has gotten the chance to do its own internal investigation. This reaction from managers in the private sector is reasonable. Nonetheless, the policy trend with more reliance on corporate compliance and self-reporting suggests a need to balance the risks associated with self-regulation with systems that encourage witnesses to react. Internal compliance may fail to prevent corruption, particularly corruption that increases corporate profits, and even if most firms operate with high ethical standards, there are managers and owners who undermine their internal compliance programs to gain from corrupt schemes. The bounty for whistle-blowing protects a company, its owners, and employees from a bribery-inclined management team, and thus there are benefits of such programs also for the private sector. The crucial element, nevertheless, is to identify the right level of compensation for whistle-blowers.

One challenge is how the specific mechanisms of corruption may render the whistle-blower program dysfunctional or cause counterintuitive effects. Schikora (2011), who conducted experimental research on this theme, explains that if both sides of the corrupt deal are encouraged to blow the whistle on proposed corruption, the game-theoretical equilibrium might very well be no whistle-blowing. Given the longer-run advantages of keeping to a corrupt scheme, "no reporting" becomes a stable equilibrium for those involved and may even strengthen the mutual trust necessary for the corruption to go on.[47] It is not clear which forms of asymmetries should be introduced in whistle-blower programs to distort this "collusion." Besides, reward systems work differently across countries and contexts. There are cultural (average) differences in how individuals adapt to norms and become motivated, and this may affect the propensity to blow the whistle. Several studies point to systematic differences between *individualistic* and *collectivistic* societies. For example, in the United States, Australia, and Norway, which are generally categorized as individualistic societies, the propensity to speak out about corruption when uncovered in one's own organization is far less dependent on a firm's internal culture and norms when compared to countries such as Thailand, China, and India, which are generally categorized as collectivistic societies. Even if sweeping generalizations about cultural variation in attitudes to corruption should be avoided, the question of whether whistle-blower programs should be adapted to their cultural context seems an important one.

Corrupt Market Players

There are similarities between individual whistle-blower reactions and the decisions of firms and organizations to react when they come across corruption committed by competitors or representatives of regulatory institutions. Firms, however, are less vulnerable to retaliation and less easily intimidated, and therefore it is a bit puzzling that firms generally have a low propensity to report, even when they are convinced that they have lost a contract because a competitor has paid a bribe. Wouldn't they have a reason to react if a competitor could be punished—particularly if this could result in cleaner tenders? The puzzle must be understood in light of the different conditions and opportunities for a company to make a profit.[48] In markets where the risk of corruption is high, antitrust oversight is generally weak and the options of profiting from cartel collaboration are significant. Such options may vanish for a firm that chooses to speak out about its competitors' (that is, potential cartel members') corruption, particularly because this would highlight corruption on the part of the procuring entity. Beyond that, the control and court systems may not be perceived as proactive and independent if corruption and collusion can go on with few, if any, consequences. Consequently, there would be no incentive for the firm to file a complaint.[49]

Instead of speaking out, the firm may benefit from combinations of corruption and other forms of offences. Lambert-Mogliansky (2011) explains how corruption and collusion are strategic complements: they generate more illegal rents for the firms involved if they combine the two, rather than use them separately. Susan Rose-Ackerman summarizes the argument as follows:

> Instead of competing with each other in the level of bribe payments, firms may organize a cartel and pay off the procurement official to keep the collusive arrangement operating, giving him a share of the excess profits from the project. If a reform simply targets the payment of kickbacks, the official has less power to extort payoffs, but the firms can still collude to share the market. If corruption is attacked with no concern for collusion, there may be no social benefits from a crackdown. An anticorruption drive might simply make the cartel cheaper and more lucrative to organize, so that the firms still present a united front that forces the state to continue overpaying for public projects. (Rose-Ackerman and Søreide 2011, xvii)

The combination of corruption and collusion is challenging, particularly in civil law–based countries where different institutions are often mandated to investigate different forms of crime, instead of searching for combinations of such offences.[50]

Most of the relevant literature on firms' propensity to speak out about their own and other market players' crimes has focused on cartel behavior, and not corruption and collusion combined. Recently, a literature on *leniency* has emerged.[51] A main finding is that leniency programs—defined as a set of rules for granting reductions in or elimination of penalties to firms or individuals who come forward with information about their involvement in crime (notably, reporting before the crime would have been revealed by investigators)—increase cartel deterrence and make law enforcement processes for each case more efficient. At the same time, there is a risk that leniency programs stabilize some cartels, given that the expected fall in prices after a case has been revealed may determine a loss higher than the gains of reporting.[52] Besides, if those who investigate such cases are busy investigating reported leniency cases, there may be fewer resources available to detect the unreported cases.[53] By help of experimental research, Bonogni et al. (2012) compare the deterrent impact of fines, leniency, and rewards, respectively. They find that while leniency programs have the expected impact of more reporting, their potential stabilizing, pro-collusive impact is voided by the reward for reporting. According to these results, leniency distorts the mutual trust needed for cartels to persist; fewer cartels get started and a relatively larger share of cartels is reported. One cannot necessarily generalize from the results of these experiments, but the results at least reveal that the specific design of leniency programs matters a lot.

Research on the propensity of players to speak out is still in its infancy, inasmuch as they are either individuals within organizations or organizations in society. As discussed, there are some useful findings, but there are also arguments that go in different directions. With a rapidly increasing literature on whistleblowing, a more solid understanding of how reactions to uncovered crime may be encouraged is likely to surface.

Political Failure

Even in well-functioning democracies, politicians can sometimes expect to sit quite safely despite their governance failures; there are numerous examples of how voters fail to replace their corrupt politicians and, in some countries, this seems to be the rule rather than the exception.[54] The political economy literature explains some of these failures.[55] One category of explanations addresses the reasons why voters may not necessarily be expected to punish bad leaders. Many cast their votes on the basis of new promises, regardless of an incumbent's past performance and are unable to see through a charismatic façade. Despite leaders' past failures, some may simply decide to cast their vote to female candidates for the sake of gender balance or to representatives of their own ethnic group. Some may support a political party because of its history and position, regardless of its leader. Besides, the party's internal recruitment process may not be particularly democratic and may be steered by elders and their allies who happen to be in control of public and private institutions. Voters who trust none of the candidates may still decide to vote simply in support of democracy.[56] Despite all these "democratic failures" to replace corrupt politicians, some results show that voters are less likely to support dishonest candidates if they are informed about the candidates' failures.[57] For voters to be informed, they must have access to information that can reveal political failure. Corrupt leaders, however, have interest in controlling what information is being released to the public. If it is impossible to deceive the voters by manipulating the release of information, elections may be rigged. If this course of action does not secure power, other stratagems can be used, including allocation of state revenues for de facto campaign finance,[58] populist spending for the most critical voters, and boosting the economy to show good results.[59] As a consequence, the incumbent's chance of winning the election without rigging the voting process increases, while the election itself becomes a substantial burden on the economy.

Difficulties in making election and parliamentary systems deliver in developing countries have triggered debates about democracy. The debate itself weakens the position of citizens because it suggests that it is no longer taken for granted that the people living in a particular geographical area should control the appointment of their leaders and the decisions they make.[60] While democracy, when it functions properly, is the clearest expression of a government's legitimacy, the core mechanism reflecting state legitimacy is related to *trust*.[61] Governing a country becomes more difficult as the ruling regime becomes less trusted. A lack of trust is typically accompanied by oppression, brutal force, press control, political imprisonment, and human rights violations. Development is accordingly hampered by transaction costs and increased investment risks. In contrast, a trusted government has lower expenses in oppression and control, a more motivated state administration, and, in dealing with corruption, is far better able to trigger norm-implementation processes through legal reform. Democratic elections are only one among several trust-building devices. Another is the function of checks and balances at the top level of governance, specifically the role of the parliament in controlling the executive and maintaining the independence of the legal systems. A country's constitution is often an ideal to strive for, but how its checks and balances work in practice is what determines how far a government can be trusted.[62] Moreover, a true (and trust-generating) concern for the well-being of a population and the framework conditions for the private sector should mean exchange of information and dialogue about challenges. Citizens must be allowed and expected to report the need for government action, better services, or targeted investments. The needed dialogue between citizens and government can take place in many different settings (including the media forums, public hearings, political meetings, civil society channels, political parties, and so on), contributing to generate the legitimacy needed for efficient anticorruption and law enforcement in general. Based on their empirical study of corruption across Chinese regions, Dong and Torgler (2012) find that a free press is important in curbing corruption in China.

The propensity of politicians to benefit from corruption depends on the democratic shortcomings discussed, the visibility of the politicians' performance, and checks on their failures; these factors affect, or are affected by, the broader moral landscape. Countries with low levels of corruption usually have well-functioning control systems, including an independent national audit office, a police force and prosecutors, a trusted tax office, sector oversight, and regulatory institutions, but they also have a free press, access to information, and provide opportunities for citizens to speak their mind and organize for political alternatives.[63] Other components include recognition of human rights, moderate income differences, and fair competition. The question, however, is not how to characterize well-functioning societies but how to help countries develop in that direction.

Notes

1. The point made in this paragraph is taken from Søreide and Williams (2014, 2). For evolutionary psychology with relevance to crime, see Dawkins (1976), Trivers (1971), Pinker (1997), Frey (2009), and Harel (2012), among others. Corruption is illegal in all countries, and several international conventions promote legal harmonization and enforcement of anticorruption legislation.

2. For the utility maximization concept, see microeconomic theory, for example, in Varian (1992) or Salvatore (2003). Gary Becker (1968) developed the concept for crime in general; Susan Rose-Ackerman (1978) for corruption specifically. For recent insights on the economics of crime, see chapters in Harel and Hylton (2012), Di Tella, Edwards, and Shardgodsky (2010), and Garoupa (2009).

3. For example, firms found guilty in corruption can be debarred from public tenders in many countries and from tenders on contracts financed by multilateral development banks. The contracts lost because of debarment may hit a firm harder than a sentence for corruption, even though many countries have raised the level of penalties in recent years.

4. This is a controversial area in research on crime, and there are even results suggesting that some detection mechanisms, which are expected to have a crime-preventing impact, can have counterintuitive effects and increase the level of corruption, see Frank and Schulze (2000) and Schulze and Frank (2003).

Drivers of Corruption • http://dx.doi.org/10.1596/978-1-4648-0401-4

5. Miceli (2012) describes the law and economics of punishment, including the trade-off between prison sentences and fines.

6. The term "elasticity" refers to the effect of longer penalties on the propensity to commit crime.

7. For literature reviews, see Eide, Rubin, and Shepherd (2006) and Harel (2012), among many others.

8. See, for example, Moore (2010) for arguments and a review on the importance of placing blame; and for an assessment of the mentioned trade-off, Arlen (2012) and Miceli (2012). There is a significant literature on both stands.

9. Different views on these questions are reflected in cross-country variation in the opportunity to hold organizations criminally liable, with a more positive attitude toward corporate responsibilities in Anglo-American law. Brickey (2012) explains the justification and background for corporate criminal responsibility.

10. For an explanation of mechanisms, see Piselli (2000) and Schooner (2004). With reference to EU procurement rules, Willaims (2006, 2009) describes mandatory exclusion and Hjelmeng and Søreide (2014) discuss principles for "self-cleaning."

11. See Leroy and Fariello (2012), Seiler and Madir (2012), Dubois (2012), and Dubois and Nowlan (2013) for explanation and facts.

12. See theories presented by Besley and McLaren (1993), Van Rijckeghem and Weder (2001), and Aidt (2003) for good examples.

13. On market position, corruption, and tender outcomes, see, among others, Ades and Di Tella (1999), Shleifer and Vishny (1993), Auriol and Blanc (2009), Celentani and Ganuza (2002), Bjorvatn and Søreide (2005, 2013), Auriol and Straub (2011), and Svensson (2003).

14. See, among others, Abbink (2006), Lambsdorff (2002a), and Jacquemet (2005).

15. Reward structures determine how talents are more or less allocated into productive/harmful activities; explained by Mehlum, Moene, and Torvik (2003, 2006) and Acemoglu (1995).

16. This is studied by Harstad and Svensson (2011) and Lambsdorff (2002b).

17. See Andvig and Moene (1990), Søreide (2009), and Djawadi and Fahr (2013), and discussion below.

18. See reviews of the literature listed in the footnote above and in the references, the study by Rose-Ackerman and Truex (2013) being among the most recent.

19. Shafir (2013), who offers comprehensive reviews of results thus far and discusses their many policy implications, does not necessarily agree; we may have to rethink decision making on too many dimensions for modifications in existing theories to work.

20. See Kahneman and Tversky (1979, 1986), chapters in Shafir (2013), and Kahneman (2011).

21. Gender differences in corruption have been debated in the literature. Dollar, Fisman, and Gatti (2001), Swamy et al. (2001), Torgler and Valev (2010), Guveneli and Sanyal (2012), and Dong and Torgler (2012) all find women to be significantly less likely to be involved in corruption and a clear correlation between women in power and low levels of corruption (causality notwithstanding), while others, such as Rivas (2008) and Abbink, Irlenbush, and Renner (2002) are less clear on such effects. Djawadi and Fahr (2013) find women to be more risk averse than men, but not more likely than men to assess the risk of detection correctly.

22. Fleming and Zyglidopoulos (2009) describe these mechanisms with references to some of the most debated corruption cases in the last decade.

23. Several authors explain how corruption can be rationalized and "normalized" by individuals and organizations. See specifically Ashforth and Anand (2003) and Rabl and Kühlman (2009).

24. Vandenabeele (2007) provides a short review of psychological explanations. In short, employees' basic psychological needs is key to understanding the impact of the institutional socialization process (or internalization); that is, the more institutions "respond" to the individual's needs, the more the individual is likely to adopt its culture and norms, even if the culture is prone to corruption.

25. This result stems from evolutionary psychology, which emphasizes the importance of family and tribe. Corruption seems more prevalent in societies with ethnic diversion, but the correlation can have several explanations. See Dong and Torgler (2012) for variation within one large country (regions in China) and Transparency International's Corruption Perceptions Index (CPI) for a cross-country picture of perceived challenges.

26. See Aspinall and Klinken (2010).

27. Examples of external patronage control over civil servants (patron-client relationships) are presented in Smith (2003) and Ekeh (1975), for example. A manager with tolerance for patron-client relationships may be more inclined to condone corruption.

28. The benevolent principal could well be the owners and society while the top executive is thought of as the agent; the theory still applies. Such theory is presented by Laffont and Tirole (1991, 1994).

29. See Aidt (2003) for a principal-agent model used to analyze the anticorruption impact of changes in wages offered, control mechanisms, and various performance-based compensations schemes.

30. Based on experimental research, Abbink (2002) finds no correlation between wage levels and the propensity to be involved in corruption. A study of Bulgaria's tax administration finds that higher wages reduce corruption, but concludes (based on extrapolation of results), that current wages would have to triple to eradicate the corruption-related challenges. See Pashev, Valev, and Pasheva (2010).

31. Research on civil servant motivation, based on alternative compensation schemes and control, are described by Weiebel, Rost, and Ostreloch (2009), Feldman (2009), Rauch and Evans (2000), and Holmstrom and Milgrom (1991) among many others. Despite different views in the literature, an important message from these authors is that simple performance pay can weaken employees' intrinsic work motivation.

32. See, for example, Park and Berry (2012) on performance-based compensation schemes introduced by the US federal government in 1978. Lindkvist (2012, 2014) provides results from Tanzania where performance schemes were found to work better as an anticorruption remedy when combined with merit-based promotions.

33. The mechanism is described by Deci (1975) as a "corruption effect."

34. For more details, see Laffont and Martimort (2001) and Pink (2010).

35. Della Porta and Vannucci (1999) underscore the importance of more weight on outcome control for anticorruption purposes.

36. We can separate between top-down corruption, where managers share benefits with their staff or allow them to take bribes to keep them loyal (whatever the manager does), and down-up corruption, where staff are in position to demand bribes (for

example, because they are the ones in contact with clients) and share the returns with the manager to keep him or her from clamping down on their illegal activities.

37. Several "solutions" for reducing this gap are described by Ross McLeod (2010, 47), a case study from Indonesia.

38. Søreide, Tostensen, and Skage (2012) provide a qualitative study of mismanagement of travel compensation systems and allowances for meeting and training attendance in three African countries, a study conducted for Norad. (For a short version, see Skage, Søreide, and Tostensen [2014]).

39. Ostrom (2000) and Olson (1996) explain this problem in different ways. While Olson points at the lack of formal structures for good collaboration and organization in society, Ostrom points at how well citizens manage to collaborate without "structures." See also Rothstein and Teorell (2008) for discussion of how collective action perspectives contribute to a better understanding of corruption. However, several case studies suggest that what appears to be a collective action challenge (that is, a coordination problem) can be a symptom of more serious dysfunctions. See, for example, Aspinall and Van Klinken (2010) and Cribb (2010) on Indonesia under Suharto, and De Oliveira (2007) on Angola.

40. A further possible reason for such priorities is state administration dysfunctions associated with "grand corruption" at political levels, discussed in section "Corrupt Market Players".

41. Consequences might include arduous court cases, lost income, work responsibilities, and career opportunities. Even if those who report are convinced that their reaction is ethically right, they know that they will not necessarily come out of it as heroes. The study by Dyck, Morse, and Zingales (2010) of whistle-blowers in US firms found that 45 percent of those who revealed cases where the firm in question was in fact found guilty kept their identity hidden. The costs of reacting with full identity were considered high even in cases when the evidence was strong enough to win the court case. Auditors who blew the whistle on evidence of fraud or corruption most certainly lost their clients.

42. Human Rights Watch keeps track of such risks worldwide. See also the website of Reporters Without Borders for their Press Freedom Barometer and an overview of violations against journalists, including murder.

43. Government support for anticorruption agencies, for example, has tended to decrease as these agencies exert greater authority (particularly if targeting political corruption). Strong political support is crucial for their performance, according to Recanatini (2011) and Batory (2012).

44. Dodd-Frank Wall Street Reform and Consumer Protection Act, July 21, 2010, Section 922. The act requires the Securities and Exchange Commission (SEC) to pay whistle-blowers a reward ranging from 10 percent to 30 percent of the monetary sanctions, provided that the information is new to the SEC and original, stems directly from the whistle-blower, and is not a result of other investigations, audits, or hearings, or part of an attempt to exploit this law.

45. See Blount and Markel (2012) for discussion of results.

46. See Dyck, Morse, and Zingale (2010) and Miceli, Near, and Dworkin (2013).

47. As discussed above, it could lead to more persistent forms of corruption. On reciprocity and corruption, see Lambsdorff (2002a, 2002b, 2007).

48. For a business survey and analysis of this hesitation to report incidences of corruption, see Søreide (2008).

49. In contrast, in countries with well-functioning institutions, a clear tendency to complain about firms' unfair benefits in tenders should be, and often is, seen.

50. Discussed by Søreide (2012) and Lambert-Mogliansky (2011).

51. For explanation of leniency, see Spagnolo (2004, 2006), Aubert, Rey, and Kovacic (2006), and Harrington (2008). Brenner (2009) finds leniency programs in Europe to have improved law enforcement efficiency because the time and resources required per cartel case has decreased significantly.

52. Hence, as Spagnolo (2004, 2006) explains, the "run to the court house" effect will increase as the incentive mechanism gets stronger.

53. See Bigoni et al. (2012) and Chang and Harrington (2008, 2012).

54. In particular, countries scoring weakly on the Democracy Index. See the website of the *Economist* Intelligence Unit

55. Explanations and reviews are provided by Besley (2006), Mueller (2003), and Persson and Tabellini (2000) among others.

56. These arguments are presented also in Søreide (2013). Moreover, in cases of high illiteracy, voters may lack even the required understanding of the purpose of voting.

57. Rose-Ackerman and Truex (2013, section IV) review relevant results. See in particular results by Weitz-Shapiro and Winters (2010) and Figueiredo, Hidalgo, and Kasahara (2010). Estache and Foucart (2013) propose initiatives to "bench-mark" politicians with the help of expert assessments of political performance, so that democratic mechanisms can be invigorated.

58. See Helle and Rakner (2014) for a study of how state revenues have been used for campaign finance in Uganda.

59. Nordhaus (1975) and Drazen (2001) explain political business cycles.

60. The idea of a social contract and accountability to the people, early described by Rousseau 1762/2004, has a particularly strong position in Western societies, but its general welfare-enhancing effects are well documented. See Feng (2003), Treisman (2007), and Knutsen (2013), who find that democracy has a positive impact on growth, even in weak-capacity states.

61. See Rose-Ackerman (2001) for an explanation of the role of trust in state-building processes with reference to postsocialist countries.

62. See Evrenk (2011) for an analysis of why even honest politicians will choose not to enforce or implement efficient anticorruption policies if doing so may threaten their comparative advantage as "the clean candidate."

63. See various democracy and human rights indicators and Transparency International's (2012) National Integrity Studies throughout Europe.

CHAPTER 4

Policy Implications
and Further Research

Making anticorruption policy choices guided by research results is difficult for several reasons. First, the knowledge base is limited and diverse. The literature on corruption has expanded rapidly over the last 10–15 years, but the methodological obstacles remain substantial and few impact evaluations have provided results of general applicability. Even experts' knowledgeable of the most up-to-date research do not know how anticorruption initiatives should optimally be designed. Second, because corruption is politically sensitive, there could be a risk that raising the issue would worsen framework conditions for development support. Dialogue on anticorruption can easily be considered an "insult" that can distort an otherwise good collaboration and possibly place other political goals at risk—not only development goals but also commercial ambitions, military strategies, and access to natural resources. A third reason relates to the fundamental position of a country's administration. The state's monopoly on decision making is a problem for outsiders who might steer a country's administrative processes in a direction perceived to be conducive to fighting corruption. Further, the high probability of failure in anticorruption policy work may have tempted some development partners to operate with diffuse anticorruption targets. This is unlikely to be a strategy to avoid criticism from evaluators, but in general, anticorruption policy work is characterized by unclear performance targets. Despite the huge amounts spent on this agenda over the last two decades, up to now donor-financed anticorruption efforts have produced few, methodologically robust impact-evaluation results.[1]

Although results of general validity are few and far between, a large amount of "approximate knowledge" on corruption has been acquired in recent decades, and corruption is far better understood than it was only 20 years ago. Increasingly, specialists are able to understand what works. Combined with substantial amounts of research on crime, integrity, rationality, authority, and criminal justice systems generally, it can be said for certain that corruption will decrease as the population increasingly perceives corruption as a moral wrong; the better informed the people who have an incentive to react, the better the systems will be that hold those involved responsible, and eventually, the more motivated government representatives will be in performing service delivery. There are numerous nuances, views, uncertainties, and policy alternatives in each of these areas, and because solutions also depend on context, there appear to be few eternal truths in anticorruption. Research increases the validity of policy recommendations, reduces disagreement on what works, and puts forward new solutions when challenges remain unresolved. While many insights from academia have been put to good use in policy work, this section points at areas where (i) anticorruption policy could possibly be made more efficient through better use of existing research results; (ii) research is progressing rapidly and likely to offer useful results soon; and (iii) more research is needed for the development of reliable anticorruption policy solutions.

Research Ignored?

Given the large good governance literature containing a variety of recommendations from different academic disciplines, policy environments should not be expected to jump on each and every research finding. However, there are areas where results have been around for a while and there are valid reasons for policy makers to look at them. Some examples follow.

Financial regulation. This is an area in anticorruption where policy environments have been slow in developing solutions, despite recommendations from research. Efficient collaboration is critical to fight not only corruption but also tax evasion, organized crime, and money laundering. It has nevertheless taken two to three decades of collaboration via the Financial Action Task Force (FATF) for governments to start harmonizing their legislation and reducing financial secrecy. The last few years have seen several successes in the development of an international legal platform for holding those involved responsible.[2] However, as Elsayyad and Konrad (2012) explain, a stepwise approach to fighting financial secrecy will be tougher in the presence of fewer remaining financial secrecy providers that profit more from their "market power." Therefore, the impact of more sophisticated legal tools depends on how they are enforced. This is particularly challenging in low-capacity environments, where the failure to recognize the damage caused by financial secrecy is widespread, and where enforcement is prevented by influential players who benefit from the status quo.[3] The opportunities to sanction the failure to comply with new rules are few, and despite a more developed legal platform, stolen assets cannot be easily recovered and returned, governments are still hesitant to share evidence and information, and financial institutions and advisers who are responsible for reporting suspicious transactions may continue to condone these crimes. This is a clear example of gatekeeper responsibility[4] coming into conflict with profit-making opportunities, as explained by Kraakman (1986), Brown (1993), and Ferrarini and Giudici (2005), among others. In none of the 216 cases of corporate fraud studied by Dyck, Morse, and Zingales (2010) was the case revealed by players at investment banks, commercial banks, or stock exchanges. Financial institution responsibilities have to match their strategic incentives as profit-maximizing players, and where this is not possible, state financial controls should be expanded.

Rentier states. When it comes to combating the risk of a resource curse, as discussed in chapter 2, political scientists have underscored the importance of having political checks and balances in play, preferably before production of oil or other resources begins. It has been argued that in practice, however, governments and the donor community have tended either to ignore oil-producing developing countries' need for support (because they will get revenues from the export of resources) or to line up to offer support for the narrow development of sector regulation[5] on the false assumption that the industry can be shaped and function best independently of the broader political environment. This is an area where the foreign policy of many developed countries is in conflict with recommendations in the development-focused literature. Even if revenues from resource production will easily bolster a corrupt government's power and position, there is not much political will among the natural-resource buyers to exert pressure on governments for legitimate rule and reduced corruption. Players in the international petroleum industry (including owners) are often serious about corporate social responsibility and their own law abidingness, which is indeed important, but they largely ignore their opportunities to influence the development of the host country. When it comes to the funds offered as development aid and loans (that is, the second rentier state dilemma addressed), there is general agreement in policy and research about the importance of coordinated, consistent, and solid public financial management systems, as expressed in the Paris Declaration of Aid Effectiveness. However, Allan (2010, 26) argues that various stakeholders tend to "provide the money anyway" and that the importance of robust public financial management (PFM) systems is still not sufficiently recognized by development partners.

Markets. Many anticorruption efforts targeted at market mechanisms are concentrated on the tender situation. Better procurement rules have been considered *the* approach for securing clean allocation of contracts, fair competition, and good price-quality combinations. However, it is known for certain that firms influence their opportunities to make a profit through a range of different channels (as discussed in the "Intentions to Fix Market Failure" section), and not only by influencing tenders. As a result, the risk of business-related corruption is more complex than what is often assumed by policy makers, and procurement procedures are easily manipulated, either through the appearance of compliance with rules or with the excuse of some extraordinary situation.[6] Many developing countries have reformed their procurement procedures over the last 15 years. Yet, in some, the result has been a too-rigid set of procedures that makes securing the best possible value for money difficult; in others, too-wide exemption clauses are often maintained, and the anticorruption impact of better procurement procedures is thus impeded. A clear message from research, however, is that fair competition is an essential anticorruption remedy (see Bliss and Di Tella [1997], Ades and Di Tella [1999], and Acemoglu and Verdier [2000]). Research also shows that corruption levels decrease as the transition toward a market economy advances and independent regulatory institutions are allowed to function well.[7] Best-practice procurement procedures are not sufficient to promote and protect competition, much less to combat tender-related corruption. Instead, the procurement rules should open for the selection of the best price-quality combination while a broader set of integrity mechanisms should be better targeted at corruption risks in public procurement tenders.

Sanctions and penalties. The importance of holding offenders responsible is often ignored by good-governance policy advisers. Penalties for corrupt behavior could be better attuned to results in the law and economics literature. In practice, fines and prison sentences for bribers tend to increase with the size of the bribe, not with the outcome of the corrupt deal. Given the principle of marginal returns (Rose-Ackerman 1978, 2010a), the higher the offender's gains, the stronger the legal reaction should be. If not, the reaction loses its preventive impact for those bribes that exceed a certain level: the net benefit for the briber will be positive, even when punished, because of the larger benefit received from committing the crime.[8] The fact that a bribe is paid in the personal economy of the bribe recipient suggests that the illegal payment can be small (yet still significant in the personal sphere of the decision maker) compared to the potential gains, but also quite detached from the size of the gains and the value of the (bought) decision. Further, the more corrupt the government representative, the less betrayal needs to be compensated with a bribe. Intuitively, the bribe can be smaller under circumstances where corruption is entrenched, as compared with the situation in which the corruption is the result of a trade-off between personal benefits (that is, the bribe) and benefits for society.[9] In other words, the size of the bribe is not a good indicator of the severity of the crime, and sentences should not be based on this assumption.

Transparency and civil society. Supporting civil society and pressuring for transparency are essentials in many donor-financed anticorruption programs, yet warnings from research regarding these issues have been ignored. Transparency initiatives are often treated as an end in themselves, but research warns that access to (state-controlled) information will not bring much change unless combined with more structural changes in control institutions and at the political level.[10] Transparency is a necessary but not sufficient condition for reaction against corruption,[11] and increased access to information must be combined with support to competent institutions that have the authority to react.[12] Multistakeholder groups, consisting of players from the private sector, civil society, and government, are often seen as a solution for the implementation of good-governance reforms.[13] In practice, however, it is difficult to make them serve in a group role because the members' incentives may go in very different directions. Power imbalances or collusion between categories of stakeholders may be brought into the group and distort its operations.[14] Arenas for dialogue between stakeholders are important, but their incentives to collaborate to achieve a common goal must be understood and not just taken for granted. There are many good intentions in transparency programs and demand for good governance, but more can be done in terms of quality control of each step between program and anticorruption impact.

Perceptions and communication. Communicating an estimated perceived extent of corruption matters to actual levels of corruption. As discussed in the "Corporate Structures and Secret Identities" section, perceptions of extensive corruption can drive corruption levels through several mechanisms. Signals of high levels of corruption affect citizens' trust in state administration and hence in the administrators' propensity to take or offer bribes. It induces business people to assume incorrectly that bribes are "needed" to secure business in the country, which "improves" the opportunity for agents to profit from the bribery and allows corruption to escalate. In addition, signals of high levels of corruption determine the players' estimated risk, in turn steering their decision to be involved. These different mechanisms should induce policy makers to communicate the high probability of meeting an *honest* decision maker, which can indeed be high even in countries where the problem of corruption is severe. Compared to civil society organizations, governments and development banks are typically more careful in how they communicate the extent of corruption, partly because of the sensitivities discussed earlier in this section. However, because nongovernmental organizations (NGOs) get more funding for anticorruption work from these same sources if they can point out more corruption, perhaps the whole development community shares responsibility for signaling (too?) high levels of corruption.

Research Frontiers

Numerous anticorruption research projects are in progress across the globe, so many policy-relevant findings will be seen in the years to come. Below are examples of areas where useful research results are expected.

Rationality. As discussed in chapter 3, there has been significant development in understanding how individuals adapt to society, respond to stimulus, and adjust to group norms. Although implications for policy work are not yet clear, many of the results place law and economics propositions in a critical light.[15] Motivations are far more complex than previously assumed, individuals are less prone to be steered by external carrots on sticks, and the consistency between an individual's goals and actions is not as obvious as was often believed. According to Bardhan (2006), oversimplified assumptions of rational or logical behavior are even more misleading when trying to understand developing countries, where state structures often lack the assumed legitimacy, actors are not as informed as assumed, and the short-term gains of informal, relation-based procedures may exceed the perceived long-term benefits of formal, unbiased decision making. Even if the literature on what appears to be irrational decision making is still fragmented, there has been progress in behavioral science and studies of cultural context, and within a few years results relevant to anticorruption can be expected. Empirical microanalysis of corruption-related phenomena is gaining ground, and as referred to in many places in this text, mechanisms of corruption are more frequently studied in controlled environments by help of experiments. There is increasing awareness of the importance of impact-evaluation field experiments, a kind of research that could bring more solid evidence on what works, at least in certain contexts.[16]

Organization. Progress has also been made on the internal life of organizations. The principal-agent theories, largely developed by Jean Tirole and his colleagues in Toulouse, have been extended for anticorruption and tested empirically, as discussed in the "Organization of State Authority" section. Organization and the allocation of responsibilities are of great importance, but it is difficult to balance control and discretion. According to Bac (1998, 101), "the lack of satisfactory formal models on public bureaucracies and supervision procedures impedes our understanding of the many organizational aspects of corruption." However, experts are now learning about relevant trade-offs and mechanisms through empirical studies of work motivation, performance, and reaction against various institutional weaknesses, including grabbing. Some caution is needed when using performance-based compensation schemes and rewards for reporting illegal acts because this is an area where experts have become aware of possible indirect negative consequences (as discussed in chapter 3). Many organizational aspects are on a good research track, even if more results are needed for the fine-tuning of anticorruption initiatives.

State legitimacy. State legitimacy seems more important for the general readiness to abide by rules than what many theories on crime have traditionally assumed. Legitimacy touches on fundamental values of identity and the position of the state, aspects that are important to individual intrinsic motivation and norm implementation. In other words, if the state behaves in a trustworthy and fair way, citizens are likely to do the same.[17] The mechanism is difficult to study empirically, because of the many other factors that correlate with a legitimate government, but at least from the perspective of experimental research, results on how individuals adapt to their framework conditions are expected. The results will help in understanding which fundamental conditions have to be fulfilled for "standard anticorruption approaches" to have their intended impact, and such insights will be useful when identifying anticorruption priorities. How state legitimacy and criminal justice systems are related is another area where useful findings are expected; but again, research results are not yet ready to be transformed into certified policy tools.[18]

Economic development. A recent study by Bai et al. (2013) questions the standard assumptions of anticorruption and development. The authors suggest that corruption can decrease as a result of better framework conditions for business. Well-functioning markets may "crowd out" corruption, and if they do, the causality between economic development and reduced corruption runs both ways. Mehlum, Moene, and Torvik (2003, 2006) describe how reduced corruption is a consequence of economic development and the presence of honest and productive alternatives. More empirical research is expected to reach a full understanding of these processes. More research is particularly needed to learn how players' strategic choices change as an economy grows, and whether the mechanisms that reduce the propensity to be involved in corruption can be enhanced. The results so far are mirrored in Khan's (2012) recent criticism of anticorruption, where he declares that good governance initiatives is not enough to secure good governance; there must also be productive jobs available and honest alternatives for earning money. Despite these insights, decision makers cannot be expected to become honest simply because an economy grows; indeed, the problem of corruption needs a well-considered strategy, but it is worth noting that some corruption may disappear as a consequence of economic development.

Research Needed

There are some policy areas that so far have evoked less attention from researchers than their policy relevance merits. Some examples follow.

Interaction. Most anticorruption initiatives are, like other anticrime initiatives, based on an assumption of individual decision making. There is a need for better understanding of group norms and the influence of groups on the individual's propensity to be involved in criminal acts. Insights into why some group contexts are more likely to produce corrupt outcomes than others will help to get out of "corruption traps" (Bobkova and Egbert 2012). How can group loyalty to corrupt schemes be broken up? In the private sector, firms and managers are held responsible for crime committed by staff members. This pragmatic, second-best solution encourages oversight and reduces the risk of scapegoats, but it fails to recognize that only the guilty should be punished. These challenges are recognized for private sector institutions. However, there might be reasons to consider similar second-best solutions for state administration if the "group-culture" is decisive for individual involvement in corruption. There are at least settings where managers in state administration could be better incentivized to combat corruption, as discussed in chapter 3, but current knowledge on how to design such schemes is far from complete.[19]

"Other" players. Most of the literature on corruption addresses the role of those who pay and/or receive bribes, but as discussed, there are more categories of players involved or who passively condone the crime. What are the roles and responsibilities of the various agents and advisors, representatives of investment banks, financial service providers, and shareholders who all may profit from successful corrupt deals, whether in the form of contracts, lower taxes, or cheap supply of input factors in production? What is the role of governments that may be too eager to see foreign market contracts awarded to "their" companies? Even if the role of these different players has often been ignored as gray zone areas, legally and/or ethically they should be understood as essential components of corrupt schemes. Transparency International has collected information about diplomatic pressure on international tenders, but there is far too little research on the role and function of "other players" involved in facilitating corruption.

Enforcement. It has now become possible in many jurisdictions to hold firms and individuals accountable for their involvement in corruption abroad.[20] However, apart from the commitment of a few countries in following up on this process, there are few court cases on cross-border bribery (Transparency International 2013). A further challenge is to control the government side of corruption in countries where the political leadership condones such crime. The international development banks sanction firms and individuals found guilty of corruption and debar them from contracts, but it has proven difficult for these international organizations to put pressure on those involved who work within or on the behalf of governments.[21] Internationally, better legal tools are available for holding decision makers accountable. This is a significant achievement, but in practice, the tools are too seldom applied (as commented in the "Research Ignored?" section). The de facto cross-border exchange of evidence needed to hold individuals and firms accountable, including between Organisation for Economic Co-operation and Development (OECD) countries, is too often inadequate. Cross-disciplinary research in political economy and law may help explain options for placing responsibility, not only for corruption but also for the failure to implement international efforts to combat corruption and other forms of crime.

Competition control. Given the strong correlation between well-functioning competition and low levels of corruption, it is important to make markets function despite corruption-related obstacles. Corruption is fought not just by searching for bribery. If market distortions are caused by corruption, it might be possible to "fight back" via fair and free competition. Competition authorities are supposed to detect illegal accumulation of industry profits, possibly caused by some form of corruption (as discussed in chapter 2), and have a role to play in collaboration with criminal law investigating units. Even if competition authorities are usually not mandated to address corruption, they should report to the police when there is reason for suspicion. The problem, particularly in civil law systems, is the use of leniency for cartel cases. Competition authorities offer leniency in exchange for information about cartels, but their offers are normally limited to violations of competition law. If cartel members cannot expect leniency for criminal law offences, it is unlikely that they will come forward when bribes have been paid. For competition authorities, it is easier to protect the leniency arrangement if their investigators concentrate on violation of competition law (which according to their mandate they should) and do not search for associated forms of crime, like corruption, which would have to entail criminal investigation. For the police, it easily becomes a Catch 22 situation because they cannot avoid investigating when they also obviously see the benefit of having cartel cases revealed. These institutional challenges are solved in various pragmatic or informal ways, but given the serious and subtle consequences of corruption in markets, as well as new results on the mechanisms of leniency (as discussed in chapter 3), more insights are needed on how to safely combine leniency and efficient criminal law enforcement, while also encouraging competition authorities to act on suspected corruption.[22]

Context and priorities. Efficient anticorruption means value for money and targeted approaches. What is seen in practice, however, is how good governance ambitions sometimes trigger a long list of anticorruption initiatives without much analysis of what is applicable to the unique challenges of a particular environment. This is not only a waste of resources; it reveals a weak understanding of what has caused the challenges and what is needed for lasting results. An oversupply of well-meant initiatives makes it difficult to generate momentum for each initiative and bears the risk of reducing honest civil servants' intrinsic motivations; it may even have a negative impact on their performance. In order to know what initiatives are needed, more research into the suspected corruption and underlying causes must be conducted. With knowledge about how corruption risks depend on institutional organization (as discussed in chapter 2), in terms of who holds what form of authority; who is controlled by whom; who is in some form of competition with whom; who is able to create what forms of shortage; and who is in what position to select, and possibly extort, clients, specialists will be better equipped to describe the specific risks and remedies. Such studies contribute to more efficient anticorruption and value for the investment over time.

Reform processes. The completion of initiated reform processes is typically less debated than the design of optimal institutions and control mechanisms, even if implementation is at least as important. In practice, a lot is known about what institutions should look like but less about how to get there. Assuming that countries could be placed in a diagram, with quality of laws and regulation on the horizontal axis and their strength of enforcement on the vertical axis, the findings would look something like figure 4.1, below, but with the name of countries listed in place of the text. Many policy initiatives seem to have been designed as if most developing countries can be placed in the northwest corner, where

Figure 4.1 Quality of Laws and Regulations in Relation to Enforcement Strength

STRENGTH OF ENFORCEMENT

Eager but without needed regulations
Countries in political change. Governments eager to reform a country with weak institutions may need support for the design of new laws and institutions.

Strong performers
Countries that easily reach international governance benchmarks. Most forms of corruption are controlled at low levels. Collusive forms of corruption are nevertheless a problem but hard to combat with laws and procedures.

Worst-case countries
Countries where citizens are caught in a poverty trap. A legal framework for better sector governance is unlikely to be implemented and enforced in the short term.

Laws in place, but not yet routine
Countries where collusion, corruption, and entrenched networks are significant challenges. Laws and procedures are often copied from OECD countries, where they work well, but are hard to enforce in practice.

QUALITY OF LAWS AND REGULATIONS

Source: World Bank; revised figures published in Søreide (2013) and Søreide and Truex (2013).
Note: OECD = Organisation for Economic Co-operation and Development.

Drivers of Corruption • http://dx.doi.org/10.1596/978-1-4648-0401-4

governments are eager to reform but just do not know how to design their institutions and write their laws. In reality, most of them are in the southeast corner, where countries already have fairly good formal rules and procedures but for a number of reasons they struggle to enforce them. Another procurement reform is rarely what these countries need to rid themselves of tender corruption; instead, they need long-term support for state building with recognition of the decisive importance of legitimate governance and good state-citizen relationships.

Solutions that look good on the drawing board may not reduce corruption if the causes are political instead of sector specific or caused by conflict and not by low capacity.[23] Reform processes are hard to complete where governments lack legitimacy, in fragile states, or where there is a general reform fatigue or weak coordination between important development partners. Research on the dynamics of reform under imperfect circumstances could improve the capacity to take into account the combination of governance failures, coordination failures, and weak framework conditions in policy decisions. The complex context for reform is rarely addressed as a separate subject in anticorruption research; however, the marginal value of more efficient strategies can be high.

Notes

1. See Poate and Vaillant (2011) for an evaluation of anticorruption strategies financed by several donor agencies. See *3ie* (http://www.3ieimpact.org/) and *J-PAL* (http://www.povertyactionlab.org) for donor-financed initiatives that are likely to bring valid results on what works.
2. See status reports, overviews of legal documents, and cases at the websites of the World Bank StAR (Stolen Asset Recovery Initiative), FATF, and the OECD.
3. See De Michele (2013) for discussion on why the impact of some international initiatives has been modest.
4. Some consultants (that is, gatekeepers) control clients' risk of involvement in fraud and corruption. However, in cases when the client benefits from the crime, the "gatekeeper" may face conflicting interests; there might be a duty to report the crime, while at the same time the value of continued collaboration with the client may encourage some to condone it—and the corruption goes undetected.
5. This is particularly the case for donor governments that host a petroleum industry, according to Kolstad, Wiig, and Williams (2009).
6. The use of exemptions is a particular challenge in emergency-related procurement. See Schultz and Søreide (2008).
7. Relevant in this context is Broadman et al. (2004), a book presenting World Bank experiences on market institutions in Southeastern Europe and further recommendations. See also Dong and Torgler (2012) on China, and Dutz and Vagliasindi (2000) on transition economies in Eastern Europe. Sandholtz and Taagepera (2005) explain corruption in transition economies as a question of survival incentives, culture, and opportunities in a communist society. Wren-Lewis (2013) presents results showing how privatization and independent regulation have reduced the effect of corruption on electricity distribution in Latin America. Independent regulation was found to be more effective than privatization.

8. See also Frey (2009).

9. For further explanation, see Bjorvatn and Søreide (2013).

10. See, for example, Buscaglia (2011) for a study of lessons learned so far from the implementation of United Nations Conference on Trade and Development.

11. Ben Olken's roads study in Indonesia (Olken 2007) is a reminder that transparency is not sufficient to react; controls must be conducted by qualified experts.

12. Developing countries often experience increased perceived corruption and decreased quality of governance in the five years following the introduction of freedom of information legislation according to studies by Costa (2012).

13. Initiatives such as Extractive Industries Transparency Initiative (EITI), Construction Sector Transparency Initiative (CoST), Kimberly, and many others are built on this model.

14. See Truex and Søreide (2011) and Søreide and Truex (2012) for studies of multistakeholder groups in construction and natural-resource production respectively.

15. See Shafir (2013) for comprehensive criticism of theories based on simplified assumptions of how humans behave.

16. For reviews of results, see Rose-Ackerman and Truex (2013), Lambsdorff (2012), Peisakhin (2011), and Banuri and Eckel (2012). See Johnsøn and Søreide (2013) for a review of methodological approaches to tell what works in anticorruption. For impact evaluation initiatives with positive impact on research and results, see *3ie* and *J-PAL* (see footnote 116).

17. Initiatives such as financial transparency or contract transparency may still matter in indirect ways; if not, citizens understand the technical details.

18. See Gloppen et al. (2010) on the courts' role in promoting political accountability in Latin America and Africa.

19. See Garoupa (2000) and Arlen (2012) for useful analyses.

20. Given important initiatives such as the US Foreign Corrupt Practices Act (FCPA) of 1977, the OECD Anti-Bribery Convention of 1999, the UN Conventions Against Corruption (2005), and the UK Anti Bribery Act of 2011.

21. The World Bank decision of holding back funding in the case of Padma Bridge in Bangladesh is an example of how remedies can be applied to put pressure on governments, despite controversy. See, for example, Sabet (2012).

22. Many civil law countries copy US legislation without realizing the importance of how their different institutional set-up differs from that of the United States. This theme was debated at the OECD Global Forum on Competition on February 27, 2014. I presented a paper on competition and corruption, available upon request.

23. Vannucci (2009) explains why Italy is a good case for studying reform failure. Many different initiatives have been introduced, and the challenges and political resistance are well documented. Vannucci points at how anticorruption successes in Italy are mostly the result of international pressure and collaboration. Reform obstacles at the political level are also discussed by Benitez, Estache, and Søreide. (2012) with reference to utilities.

CHAPTER 5

Conclusion

Empirical results, from the most micro-level studies to cross-country statistics, consistently show that corruption impedes development. It distorts political priorities, inflates prices, weakens performance, and increases transaction costs for citizens and firms. Stolen state revenues and an undersized tax base prevent developing countries from providing essential public services and reduce their ability to create the institutional framework needed to attract foreign business and develop well-functioning industries.

This report reviews how drivers of corruption are explained in the literature. Corrupt assets can be generated and grabbed in many different ways. This review describes how profits are created through market failure and the external rents from the export of natural resources and foreign aid; how the opportunity to commit a crime is improved with a hidden identity; and how the risk of power misuse depends on bureaucratic organization, while the lack of reliable estimates on the extent of corruption may in fact provide players with opportunities for corrupt revenues. Whether such opportunities for corruption are exploited depends not only on the individual but also on the institutional and moral environment, and, especially, on the extent to which this environment allows corruption to endure. The performance of corrupt civil servants is difficult to observe, but there are also managers who do not want to control them; they let the corruption go on. Many factors, such as culture, market mechanisms, and politics in particular, explain why corruption persists. The problem also depends on the way in which law enforcement systems function; in many countries, the law enforcement system is itself ingrained with corruption, thus hampering any attempt to clamp down on corruption and to strengthen anticorruption norms by holding those involved responsible.

The development community and governments around the world have made huge efforts to address corruption in the last two decades. Anticorruption is now on the political agenda in most countries, formal and informal controls have improved, and the space for conducting corrupt acts has shrunk. Laws and international formal agreements required for holding those involved responsible are largely in place, and governments in all regions are now about to enforce these tools. However, corruption persists because actors with authority profit and the risks cannot be completely eradicated. It goes high up in governance systems and inflicts national as well as international politics. Constant awareness of how strategies against corruption can be made more efficient is required, and governments, organizations, and state institutions should draw on the knowledge at hand. Efforts to explain corruption and how to fight it require insights in many different facets of society. Cross-disciplinary collaboration is needed to advance this agenda, because solutions require understanding of such topics as an individual's psychology, framework conditions, formal and informal structures and norms, organizations in the private and public sector, and legal aspects. This report identifies areas where research can be better used and where closer collaboration between academia and policy can improve strategies. Nevertheless, research and policy work are progressing for better anticorruption. With strong political leadership and prodevelopment aspirations, it should be possible to move the agenda further and achieve concrete results.

Bibliography

Abbink, K. 2002. "Fair Salaries and the Moral Costs of Corruption." Working Paper no. CeDEx 2002–05, University of Nottingham.

———. 2004. "Staff Rotation as an Anticorruption Policy: An Experimental Study." *European Journal of Political Economy* 20 (4): 877–906.

———. 2006. "Laboratory Experiments on Corruption." In *International Handbook on the Economics of Corruption*, edited by S. Rose-Ackerman. Cheltenham, UK, and Northampton, MA: Edward Elgar.

Abbink, K., B. Irlenbusch, and E. Renner. 2002. "An Experimental Bribery Game." *Journal of Law, Economics and Organization* 18 (2): 428–54.

Abed, G. T., and S. Gupta, eds. 2002. *Governance, Corruption and Economic Performance.* Washington, DC: International Monetary Fund.

Acemoglu, D. 1995. "Reward Structures and the Allocation of Talent." *European Economic Review* 39 (1): 17–33.

Acemoglu, D., and T. Verdier. 2000. "The Choice between Market Failures and Corruption." *American Economic Review* 90 (1): 194–211.

Ackerman, B., and I. Ayres. 2004. *Voting with Dollars: A New Paradigm for Campaign Finance.* New Haven, CT: Yale University Press.

Ades, A., and R. Di Tella. 1999. "Rents, Competition and Corruption." *American Economic Review* 89 (4): 982–93.

Aidt, T. S. 2003. "Economic Analysis of Corruption: A Survey." *Economic Journal* 113 (491): 632–52.

———. 2009. "Corruption, Institutions, and Economic Development." *Oxford Review of Economic Economic Policy* 25 (2): 271–91.

———. 2011. "Corruption and Sustainable Development." In *The International Handbook on the Economics of Corruption.* Vol. 2, edited by S. Rose-Ackerman and T. Søreide. Cheltenham, UK, and Northampton, MA: Edward Elgar.

AIV. 2013. "Crime, Corruption and Instability: An Exploratory Report." Report no. 85, Advisory Council on International Affairs, The Hague.

Akerele, D., and K. Gidado. 2003. "The Risks and Constraints in the Implementation of PFI/PPP in Nigeria." In *19th Annual ARCOM Conference, 3–5 September 2003, University of Brighton.* Vol. 1, edited by D. J. Greenwood, 379–91. Salford, UK: Association of Researchers in Construction Management.

Alatas, V., L. Cameron., A. Chaudhuri, N. Erkal, and L. Gangadharan. 2009a. "Gender, Culture, and Corruption: Insights from an Experimental Analysis." *Southern Economic Journal* 75 (3): 663–80.

———. 2009b. "Subject Pool Effects in a Corruption Experiment: A Comparison of Indonesian Public Servants and Indonesian Students." *Experimental Economics* 12 (1): 113–32.

Albertson, K., and C. Fox. 2012. *Crime and Economics: An Introduction.* London: Routledge.

Al-Kasim, F., T. Søreide, and A. Williams. 2008. "Grand Corruption in the Regulation of Oil." U4 Issue Paper no. 2: 2008, U4 AntiCorruption Resource Centre, Chr. Michelsen Institute, Bergen.

Allan, B. 2010. "The Paris Declaration after 2010: Resolving Collective Action Dilemmas in Public Financial Management Reform." Draft paper available at Social Science Research Network, SSRN no.1540284.

Andvig, J. C. 2012. "Public Procurement and Organized Crime—Illustrated with Examples from Bulgaria, Italy and Norway." NUPI Working Paper no. 813, Norwegian Institute of International Affairs, Oslo.

Andvig, J. C., and T. Barasa. 2014. "Grabbing by Strangers: Crime and Policing in Kenya." In *Corruption, Grabbing and Development: Real World Challenges,* edited by T. Søreide and A. Williams. Cheltenham, UK, and Northampton, MA: Edward Elgar.

Andvig, J. C., and K. O. Moene. 1990. "How Corruption May Corrupt." *Journal of Economic Behavior and Organization* 13 (1): 63–76.

Appiah, K. A. 2008. *Experiments in Ethics.* Cambridge, MA: Harvard University Press.

Arlen, J. 2011. "Failure of the Organizational Sentencing Guidelines." *The University of Miami Law Review* 66 (2): 321–62.

———. 2012. "Corporate Criminal Liability: Theory and Evidence." In *Research Handbook on the Economics of Criminal Law,* edited by A. Harel and K. N. Hylton. Cheltenham, UK, and Northampton, MA: Edward Elgar.

Armantier, O., and A. Boly. 2009. "Can Corruption Be Studied in the Lab? Comparing a Field and a Lab Experiment." CIRANO-Scientific Publications, September 1, 2008, available at Social Science Research Network. http://ssrn.com/abstract=1324120.

Ashforth, B., and V. Anand. 2003. "The Normalization of Corruption in Organizations." *Research in Organizational Behavior* 25: 1–52.

Aspinall, E., and G. van Klinken, eds. 2010. *The State and Illegality in Indonesia.* Leiden: KITLV Press.

Aubert, C., P. Rey, and W. E. Kovacic. 2006. "The Impact of Leniency and Whistleblowing Programs on Cartels." *International Journal of Industrial Organization* 24 (6): 1241–66.

Auriol, E. 2014. "Capture for the Rich, Extortion for the Poor." Working paper (forthcoming), University of Toulouse.

Auriol, E., and A. Blanc. 2009. "Capture and Corruption in Public Utilities: The Cases of Water and Electricity in Sub-Saharan Africa." *Utilities Policy* 17 (2): 203–16.

Auriol, E., and S. Straub. 2011. "Privatization of Rent-Generating Industries and Corruption." In *International Handbook on the Economics of Corruption.* Vol. 2, edited by S. Rose-Ackerman and T. Søreide. Cheltenham, UK, and Northampton, MA: Edward Elgar.

Bac, M. 1998. "The Scope, Timing and Type of Corruption." *International Review of Law and Economics* 18 (1): 101–20.

Bai, J., S. Jayachandran, E. J. Malesky, and B. A. Olken. 2013. "Does Economic Growth Reduce Corruption? Theory and Evidence from Vietnam." Unpublished manuscript. http://www.nber.org/papers/w19483.

Banuri, S., and C. Eckel. 2012. "Experiments in Culture and Corruption." Policy Research Working Paper no. 6064, Impact Evaluation Series, no. 56, World Bank, Washington, DC.

Bardhan, P. 2006. "The Economist's Approach to the Problem of Corruption." *World Development* 34 (2): 341–48.

Barma, N. H., K. A. Kaiser, T. Minh Le, and L. Viñuela. 2011. *Rents to Riches? The Political Economy of Natural Resource-led Development.* Washington, DC: World Bank.

Batory, A. 2012. "Political Cycles and Organizational Life Cycles: Delegation to Anticorruption Agencies in Central Europe." *Governance* 25 (4): 639–60.

Becker, G. 1968. "Crime and Punishment: An Economic Approach." *Journal of Political Economy* 76: 169–217.

Becker, G., and G. Stigler. 1974. "Law Enforcement, Malfeasance and the Compensation of Enforcers." *Journal of Legal Studies* 3: 1–19.

Bel, G., A. Estache, and R. Foucart. 2014. "Transport Infrastructure Failures in Spain: Mismanagement and Incompetence, or Political Capture?" In *Corruption, Grabbing and Development: Real World Challenges,* edited by T. Søreide and A. Williams. Cheltenham, UK, and Northampton, MA: Edward Elgar.

Benitez, D., A. Estache, and T. Søreide. 2010. "Infrastructure Policy and Governance Failures." CMI Working Paper no. WP 2012:5, Chr. Michelsen Institute, Bergen.

Berkowitz, D., K. Pisthor, and J. F. Richard. 2003. "Economic Development, Legality and the Transplant Effect." *European Economic Review* 47 (1): 165–95.

Bertrand, M., S. Djankov, R. Hanna, and S. Mullainathan. 2007. "Obtaining a Driver's License in India: An Experimental Approach to Studying Corruption." *The Quarterly Journal of Economics* 122 (4): 1639–76.

Besley, T. 2006. *Principled Agents? The Political Economy of Good Government.* Lindahl Lectures Series. Oxford: Oxford University Press.

Besley, T., and J. McLaren. 1993. "Taxes and Bribery: The Role of Wage Incentives." *Economic Journal* 103 (416): 119–41.

Bhagwati, J. N. 1982. "Directly Unproductive, Profit-seeking (DUP) Activities." *Journal of Political Economy* 90 (5): 988–1002.

Bigoni, M., S. O. Fridolfsson, C. Le Coq, and G. Spagnolo. 2012. "Fines, Leniency, and Rewards in Antitrust." *The RAND Journal of Economics* 43 (2): 368–90.

Bjorvatn, K., and T. Søreide. 2005. "Corruption and Privatization." *European Journal of Political Economy* 21 (1): 903–14.

———. 2013. "Corruption and Competition for Natural Resources." *International Tax and Public Finance* (forthcoming).

Black, B., R. Kraakman, and A. Tarassova. 2000. "Russian Privatization and Corporate Governance: What Went Wrong?" *Stanford Law Review* 52: 1731–808.

Bliss, C., and R. Di Tella. 1997. "Does Competition Kill Corruption?" *Journal of Political Economy* 105 (5): 1001–23.

Blount, J., and S. Markel. 2012. "The End of the Internal Compliance World as We Know It, Or an Enhancement of the Effectiveness of Securities Law Enforcement? Bounty Hunting Under the Dodd-Frank Act's Whistleblower Provisions." *Fordham Journal of Corporate and Financial Law* 17: 1023–61.

Bobkova, N., and H. Egbert. 2012. "Corruption Investigated in the Lab: A Survey of the Experimental Literature." *International Journal of Latest Trends in Finance and Economic Sciences* 2 (4): 337–49.

Bonogni, M., S. O. Fridolfsson, C. Le Coq, and G. Spagnolo. 2012. "Fines, Leniency, and Rewards in Antitrust." *Rand Journal of Economics* 43 (2): 368 90.

Bracking, S. 2012. "Secrecy Jurisdictions and Economic Development in Africa: The Role of Sovereign Spaces of Exception in Producing Private Wealth and Public Poverty." *Economy and Society* 41 (4): 615–37.

Brautigam, D. A., M. Moore, and O. Fjeldstad. 2008. *Taxation and State-Building in Developing Countries: Capacity and Consent.* Cambridge: Cambridge University Press.

Bray, J. 2005. "The Use of Intermediaries and Other Alternatives to Bribery." In *The New Institutional Economics of Corruption,* edited by J. G. Lambsdorff, M. Taube, and M. Schramm. London: Routledge.

Brenner, S. 2009. "An Empirical Study of the European Corporate Leniency Program." *International Journal of Industrial Organization* 27 (6): 639–45.

Brickey, K. 2012. "Perspectives on Corporate Criminal Liability. Perspectives on Corporate Criminal Liability." In *Encyclopedia of Criminology and Criminal Justice.* New York: Springer.

Broadman, H. G., J. Anderson, C. J. Claessens, R. Ryterman, S. Slavona, M. Vagliasindi, and G. A. Vincelett. 2004. *Building Market Institutions in South Eastern Europe: Comparative Prospects for Investment and Private Sector Development.* Washington, DC: World Bank.

Brody, R. G., J. M. Coulter, and S. Lin. 1999. "The Effect of National Culture on Whistle-Blowing Perceptions." *Teaching Business Ethics* 3 (4): 385–400.

Brown, G. H. 1993. "Financial Institution Lawyers as Quasi-Public Enforcers." *Georgetown Journal of Legal Ethics* 7: 637–724.

Brunetti, A., and B. Weder. 2003. "A Free Press Is Bad News for Corruption." *Journal of Public Economics* 87 (7–8): 1801–24.

Buchanan, J. M., R. D. Tollison, and G. Tullock, eds. 1980. *Toward a Theory of the Rent-Seeking Society.* College Station, TX: Texas A&M University Press.

Buscaglia, E. 2011. "On Best and Not So Good Practices for Addressing High-level Corruption Worldwide: An Empirical Assessment." In *International Handbook on the Economics of Corruption.* Vol. 2, edited by S. Rose-Ackerman and T. Søreide. Cheltenham, UK, and Northampton, MA: Edward Elgar.

Cameron, L., A. Chaudhuri, N. Erkal, and L. Gangadharan. 2009. "Propensities to Engage in and Punish Corrupt Behavior: Experimental Evidence from Australia, India, Indonesia and Singapore." *Journal of Public Economics* 93 (7): 843–51.

Campos, F. N., and F. Giovanni. 2008. "Lobbying, Corruption and Other Banes." Discussion Paper no. 6962, Centre for Economic Policy Research, London.

Campos, J. E. L., and S. Pradhan, eds. 2007. *The Many Faces of Corruption: Tracking Vulnerabilities at the Sector Level.* Washington, DC: World Bank.

Celentani, M., and J. J. Ganuza. 2002. "Corruption and Competition in Procurement." *European Economic Review* 46 (7): 1273–03.

Chang, M. H., and J. E. Harrington. 2008. "The Impact of a Corporate Leniency Program on Antitrust Enforcement and Cartelization (No. 548)." Working Papers, Johns Hopkins University, Department of Economics.

———. 2012. "Endogenous Antitrust Enforcement in the Presence of a Corporate Leniency Program." Unpublished data.

Charron, N. 2011. "Exploring the Impact of Foreign Aid on Corruption: Has the 'Anti Corruption Movement' Been Effective?" *Developing Economies* 49 (1): 66–88.

Chin, K. 2003. *Organized Crime, Business and Politics in Taiwan.* Armonk, NY: M. E. Sharpe.

Chong, A., A. De La O, D. Karlan, and L. Wantchekon. 2010. "Information Dissemination and Local Government's Electoral Returns: Evidence from a Field Experiment in Mexico." Unpublished paper, Yale University, New Haven, CT.

Christensen, J. 2012. "The Hidden Trillions: Secrecy, Corruption, and the Offshore Interface." *Crime, Law and Social Change* 57 (3): 325–43.

Chua, Y. T. 1999. *Robbed: An Investigation of Corruption in Philippine Education.* Quezon City: Philippine Center for Investigative Journalism.

Clapham, C. 1985. *Third World Politics: An Introduction.* London: Routledge.

Collier, P., R. Van der Ploeg, M. Spence, and A. J. Venables. 2009. "Managing Resource Revenues in Developing Economies." Oxford Centre for the Analysis of Resource Rich Economies, Oxford.

Corkin, L. 2011. "China and Angola: Strategic Partnership or Marriage of Convenience." *Angola Brief* 1 (1), Chr. Michelsen Institute (CMI), Bergen, and Centro de Estudos e Investigação (CEIC), Luanda, Angola.

Costa, S. 2012. "Do Freedom of Information Laws Decrease Corruption?" *Journal of Law, Economics and Organization* 29 (6): 1317–43.

Cribb, R. 2010. "A System of Exemptions: Historicizing State Illegality in Indonesia." In *The State and Illegality in Indonesia,* edited by E. Aspinall and G. van Klinken. Leiden: KITLV Press.

Dal Bo, E. 2006. "Regulatory Capture: A Review." *Oxford Review of Economic Policy* 22 (2): 203–25.

Dawkins, R. 1976. *The Selfish Gene.* Oxford: Oxford University Press.

Deci, E. L. 1975. *Intrinsic Motivation.* New York: Plenum.

De Figueiredo, M. F., F. D. Hidalgo, and Y. Kasahara. 2011. When Do Voters Punish Corrupt Politicians? Experimental Evidence from Brazil. Unpublished manuscript, University of California Berkeley.

Della Porta, D., and A. Vannucci. 1999. *Corrupt Exchanges: Actors, Resources, and Mechanisms of Political Corruption.* Hawthorne, NY: Aldine de Gruyter.

Del Monte, A., and E. Papagni. 2007. "The Determinants of Corruption in Italy: Regional Panel Data Analysis." *European Journal of Political Economy* 23 (2): 379–96.

De Michele, R. 2013. "How Can International Financial Institutions Support Countries' Efforts to Prevent Corruption under International Treaties and Agreements?" In *Anticorruption policy: Can International Actors Play a Constructive Role?* edited by S. Rose-Ackerman and P. Carrington. Durham, NC: Carolina Academic Press.

De Oliveira, R. S. 2007. "Business Success, Angola-Style: Postcolonial Politics and the Rise of Sonangol." *Journal of Modern African Studies* 45 (4): 595–619.

De Soto, E. 1989. *The Other Path: The Invisible Revolution in the Third World*. New York: HarperCollins.

De Valence, G. 2011. "Competition and Barriers to Entry in the Construction Industry. Modern Construction Economics: Theory and Application." In *Modern Construction Economics: Theory and Application*, edited by G. de Valence. New York: Taylor and Francis.

De Willebois, E. V. D. D., J. C. Sharman, R. Harrison, J. W. Park, and E. Halter. 2011. *The Puppet Masters: How the Corrupt Use Legal Structures to Hide Stolen Assets and What to Do About It*. Washington, DC: World Bank. http://star.worldbank.org/star/publication/puppet-masters.

Di Tella, R., S. Edwards, and E. Schardgodsky. 2010. *The Economics of Crime: Lessons For and From Latin America*. Chicago: University of Chicago Press.

Djankov, S., R. La Porta, F. Lopez-de-Silanes, and A. Shleifer. 2003. "Courts." *Quarterly Journal of Economics* 118 (2): 453–517.

Djawadi, B. M., and R. Fahr. 2013. "The Impact of Risk Perception and Risk Attitudes on Corrupt Behavior: Evidence from Petty Corruption Experiment." IZA Discussion Paper no. 7383, Insitute for the Study of Labor, Bonn.

Doig, A., and D. Norris. 2012. "Improving Anticorruption Agencies as Organisations." *Journal of Financial Crime* 19 (3): 255–73.

Dollar, D., R. Fisman, and R. Gatti. 2001. "Are Women Really the 'Fairer' Sex? Corruption and Women in Government." *Journal of Economic Behavior and Organization* 46 (4): 423–29.

Dong, B., and B. Torgler. 2012. "Causes of Corruption: Evidence from China." *China Economic Review* 26: 152–69.

Drazen, A. 2000. *Political Economy in Macroeconomics*. Princeton, NJ: Princeton University Press.

———. 2001. "The Political Business Cycle after 25 Years." In *NBER Macroeconomics Annual 2000*. Vol. 15. Cambrdige, MA: MIT Press.

Drugov, M., J. Hamman, and D. Serra. 2011. "Intermediaries in Corruption: An Experiment." *Experimental Economics*: 1 22.

Dubois, P. H. 2012. "Domestic and International Administrative Tools to Combat Fraud & Corruption: A Comparison of US Suspension and Debarment with the World Bank's Sanctions System." *University of Chicago Legal Forum*: 195–463.

Dubois, P. H., and E. Nowlan. 2013. "Global Administrative Law and the Legitimacy of Sanctions Regimes in International Law." Chapter 13 in *Anti-Corruption Policy: Can International Actors Play a Constructive Role?* edited by S. Rose-Ackerman and P. Carrington. Durham, NC: Carolina Academic Press.

Durlauf, S. N., and D. S. Nagin. 2010. The Deterrent Effect of Imprisonment." In *Controlling Crime: Strategies and Tradeoffs*, edited by P. J. Cook, J. Ludwig, and J. McCrary. Chicago: University of Chicago Press.

———. 2011. "Overview of 'Imprisonment and Crime: Can Both Be Reduced?'" *Criminology & Public Policy* 10 (1): 9–12.

Dušek, L., A. Ortmann, and L. Lizal. 2005. "Understanding Corruption and Corruptibility through Experiments: A Primer." *Prague Economic Papers* 2: 147–62.

Dutz, M., and M. Vagliasindi. 2000. "Competition Policy Implementation in Transition Economies: An Empirical Assessment." *European Economic Review* 44 (4–6): 762–72.

Dyck, A., A. Morse, and L. Zingales. 2010. "Who Blows the Whistle on Corporate Fraud?" *Journal of Finance* 65 (6): 2213–53.

Eide, E., P. H. Rubin, and J. M. Shepherd. 2006. "Economics of Crime." *Foundations and Trends in Microeconomics* 2 (3): 205–79.

Ekeh, P. 1975. "Colonialism and the Two Publics in Africa: A Theoretical Statement." *Comparative Studies in Society and History* 17 (1): 91–112.

Elsayyad, M., and K. A. Konrad. 2012. "Fighting Multiple Tax Havens." *Journal of International Economics* 86 (2): 295–305.

Engel, C., S. J. Goerg, and G. Yu. 2012. "Symmetric vs Asymmetric Punishment Regimes for Bribery." Preprint no. 2012/1, Max Planck Institute for Research on Collective Goods, Bonn.

Erwin, P. M. 2010. "Corporate Codes of Conduct: The Effects of Code Content and Quality on Ethical Performance." *Journal of Business Ethics* 99 (4): 535–48.

Estache, A., ed. 2011. *Emerging Issues in Competition, Collusion, and Regulation of Network Industries.* London: Centre for Economic Policy Research.

Estache, A., and R. Foucart. 2013 "Benchmarking Politicians." Discussion Paper Series, no. 9468, Centre for Economic Policy Research, London.

Estache, A., and C. Philippe. 2012. "The Impact of Private Participation in Infrastructure in Developing Countries: Taking Stock of about 20 Years of Experience." ECARES working paper, European Center for Advanced Research in Economics and Statistics, Brussels.

Estache, A., and L. Wren-Lewis. 2009. "Toward a Theory of Regulation for Developing Countries: Following Jean-Jacques Laffont's Lead." *Journal of Economic Literature* 47 (3): 729–70.

Evrenk, H. 2011. "Why a Clean Politician Supports Dirty Politics: A Game-Theoretical Explanation for the Persistance of Political Corruption." *Journal of Economic Behavior and Organization* 80 (3): 498–510.

Falk, A., and U. Fischbacher. 2002. "'Crime' in the Lab-Detecting Social Interaction." *European Economic Review* 46 (4–5): 859–69.

Falkingham, J. 2004. "Poverty, Out-of-Pocket Payments and Access to Health Care: Evidence from Tajikistan." *Social Science and Medicine* 58 (2): 247–58.

Feldman, Y. 2009. "The Incentives Matrix: The Comparative Effectiveness of Rewards, Liabilities, Duties and Protections for Reporting Illegality." Mimeo. http://works.bepress.com/yuval_feldman/1/.

Feldman, Y., and O. Lobel. 2009. "Incentives Matrix: The Comparative Effectiveness of Rewards, Liabilities, Duties, and Protections for Reporting Illegality." *Texas Law Review* 88: 1151.

Feng, Y. 2003. *Democracy, Governance, and Economic Performance: Theory and Evidence.* Cambridge, MA: MIT Press.

Ferrarini, G. A., and P. Giudici 2005. "Financial Scandals and the Role of Private Enforcement: The Parmalat Case." ECGI Law Working Paper no. 40/2005, European Corporate Governance Institute, Brussels.

Ferraz, C., and F. Finan. 2011. "Electoral Accountability and Corruption: Evidence from the Audits of Local Governments." *American Economic Review* 191 (4): 1274–311.

Findley, M., D. Nielson, and J. Sharman. 2012. "Global Shell Games: Testing Money Launderers' and Terrorist Financiers' Access to Shell Companies." Political Economy and Development Lab, Brigham Young University.

Fisman, R., and J. Svensson. 2007. "Are Corruption and Taxation Really Harmful to Growth? Firm Level Evidence." *Journal of Development Economics* 83 (1): 63–75.

Fjeldstad, O. H. 2003. "Fighting Fiscal Corruption: Lessons from the Tanzania Revenue Authority." *Public Administration and Development* 23 (2): 165–75.

Fleming, P., and S. C. Zyglidopoulos. 2009. *Charting Corporate Corruption: Agency, Structure and Escalation.* Cheltenham, UK, and Northampton, MA: Edward Elgar.

Flyvbjerg, B., N. Bruzelius, and W. Rothengatter. 2003. *Megaprojects and Risk: An Anatomy of Ambition.* Cambridge: Cambridge University Press.

Flyvbjerg, B., and E. Molloy. 2011. "Delusion, Deception and Corruption in Major Infrastructure Projects: Causes, Consequences and Cures." In *International Handbook on the Economics of Corruption.* Vol. 2, edited by S. Rose-Ackerman and T. Søreide. Cheltenham, UK, and Northampton, MA: Edward Elgar.

Frank, B., and G. Schulze. 2000. "Does Economics Make Citizens Corrupt?" *Journal of Economic Behavior and Organization* 43 (1): 101–13.

Frankel, J. A. 2010. "The Natural Resource Curse: A Survey." NBER Working Paper no. 15836, National Bureau of Economic Research, Cambridge, MA.

Frey, B. S. 1997. *Not Just for the Money: An Economic Theory of Motivation.* Cheltenham, UK, and Northampton, MA: Edward Elgar.

Frey, B. S. 2009. "Punishment—and Beyond." CESifo Working Paper no. 2706, Center for Economic Studies (CES), Munich; Ifo Institute, Munich; and Munich Society for the Promotion of Economic Research.

Garoupa, N. 2000. "Corporate Criminal Law and Organization Incentives: A Managerial Perspective." *Managerial and Decision Economics* 21 (6): 243–52.

———, ed. 2009. *Criminal Law and Economics.* Vol. 3 of *Encyclopedia of Law and Economics.* 2nd ed. Cheltenham, UK, and Northampton, MA: Edward Elgar.

Garoupa, N., and F. Gomez-Pomar. 2004. "Punish Once or Punish Twice: A Theory of the Use of Criminal Sanctions in Addition to Regulatory Penalties. *American Law and Economics Review* 6 (2): 410–33.

Garoupa, N., and F. Stephen. 2006. "Law and Economics of Plea-Bargaining." Draft paper available at Social Science Research Network, SSRN no. 917922.

———. 2008. "Why Plea-Bargaining Fails to Achieve Results in So Many Criminal Justice Systems: A New Framework for Assessment." *Maastricht Journal of European and Comparative Law* 15 (3): 323–58.

Global Witness. 2009. *Undue Diligence: How Banks Do Business with Corrupt Regimes.* London: Global Witness.

Gloppen, S., B. M. Wilson, R. Gargarella, and E. Skaar. 2010. *Courts and Power in Latin America and Africa.* New York: Palgrave Macmillan, 2010.

Goette, L., D. Huffman, and S. Meier. 2006. "The Impact of Group Membership on Cooperation and Norm Enforcement: Evidence Using Random Assignment to Real Social Groups." *American Economic Review Papers and Proceedings* 96 (2): 212–16.

Gong, T. 2002. "Dangerous Collusion: Corruption as a Collective Venture in Contemporary China." *Communist and Post-Communist Studies* 35 (1): 85–103.

Gordon, R. K. 2009. *Laundering the Proceeds of Pblic Sector Corruption.* Washington, DC: World Bank.

Grossman, G. M., and E. Helpman. 2001. *Special Interest Politics.* Cambridge, MA: MIT Press.

Guasch, J. L. 2004. *Granting and Renegotiating Infrastructure Concessions: Doing It Right.* Washington, DC: World Bank.

Guveneli, T., and R. Sanyal. 2012. "Perception and Understanding of Bribery in International Business." *Ethics & Behavior* 22 (5): 333–48.

Harel, A. 2012. "Economic Analysis of Criminal Law: A Survey." In *Research Handbook on the Economics of Criminal Law,* edited by I. A. Harel and K. N. Hylton. Cheltenham, UK, and Northampton, MA: Edward Elgar.

Harel, A., and K. N. Hylton. 2012. *Research Handbook on the Economics of Criminal Law.* Cheltenham, UK, and Northampton, MA: Edward Elgar.

Harrington, J. 2008. "Optimal Corporate Leniency Programs." *Journal of Industrial Economics* 56 (2): 215–46.

Harstad, B., and J. Svensson. 2011. "Bribes, Lobbying and Development." *American Political Science Review* 105 (1): 46–63.

Hasker, K., and C. Okten. 2008. "Intermediaries and Corruption." *Journal of Economic Behavior and Organization* 67 (1): 103–15.

Heidenheimer, A. J., and M. Johnston, eds. 2002. *Political Corruption: Concepts and Contexts.* 3rd ed. Piscataway, NJ: Transaction.

Helle, J. E., and L. Rakner. 2014. "'Grabbing' an Election: Abuse of State Resources in the 2011 Elections in Uganda." In *Corruption, Grabbing and Development: Real World Challenges,* edited by T. Søreide and A. Williams. Cheltenham, UK, and Northampton, MA: Edward Elgar.

Hjelmeng, E., and T. Søreide. 2014. "Debarment in Public Procurement: Rationales and Realization." In *Integrity and Efficiency in Sustainable Public Contracts,* edited by G. M. Racca and C. R. Yukins. Brussels: Bruylant.

Hodler, R. 2009. "Industrial Policy in an Imperfect World." *Journal of Development Economics* 90 (1): 85–93.

Holmstrom, B., and P. Milgrom. 1991. "Multitask Principal-Agent Analyses: Incentive Contracts, Asset Ownership, and Job Design." *Journal of Law, Economics, and Organization* 7 (special issue): 24–52.

Høyland, B., K. O. Moene, and F. Willumsen. 2012. "The Tyranny of International Index Rankings." *Journal of Development Economics* 97 (1): 1–14.

Humphreys, M., J. D. Sachs, and J. E. Stiglitz, eds. 2007. *Escaping the Resource Curse.* New York: Columbia University Press.

Hussman, J. C., and K. Rivillas. 2014. "Financial Blood-letting in the Colombian Health System: Analysis of the Systemic Rent-seeking in the Use of a Health Insurance Fund. In *Corruption, Grabbing and Development: Real World Challenges,* edited by T. Søreide and A. Williams. Cheltenham, UK, and Northampton, MA: Edward Elgar.

Jacquemet, N. 2005. "Corruption as Betrayal: Experimental Evidence on Corruption under Delegation." Working paper, Lyon II Université.

Jansen, E. G. 2014. "'Don't Rock the Boat': Why It Is So Difficult for Norway to Deal with Corruption in Development Aid Programmes." In *Corruption, Grabbing and*

Development: Real World Challenges, edited by T. Søreide and A. Williams. Cheltenham, UK, and Northampton, MA: Edward Elgar.

Johannesen, N., and G. Zucman. 2012. "The End of Bank Secrecy? An Evaluation of the G20 Tax Haven Crackdown." Working Paper no. 2012/4, Paris School of Economics, Paris.

Jøhnson, J., and T. Søreide. 2013. "Methods for Learning What Works and Why in Anticorruption." U4 Issue Paper no. 8:2013, U4 Anticorruption Resource Centre, Chr. Michelsen Institute, Bergen.

Joly, E. 2007. *Justice Under Siege: One Woman's Battle against a European Oil Company*. London: Arcadia.

Kahneman, D. 2011. *Thinking, Fast and Slow*. New York: Farrar, Straus and Giroux.

Kahneman, D., and A. Tversky. 1979. "Prospect Theory: An Analysis of Decision-making under Risk." *Econometrica* 47 (2): 263–91.

———. 1986. "Rational Choice and the Framing of Decisions. *Journal of Business* 59 (4): 251–78.

Kaufmann, D. 2003. "Rethinking Governance: Empirical Lessons Challenge Orthodoxy." In *Global Competitiveness Report 2002–2003*. Geneva: World Economic Forum.

Kenny, C. 2009. "Measuring Corruption in Infrastructure: Evidence from Transition and Developing Countries." *The Journal of Development Studies* 45 (3): 314–32.

———. 2011. *Getting Better: Why Global Development Is Succeeding—And How We Can Improve the World Even More*. New York: Basic.

Khan, M. H. 2006. "Determinants of Corruption in Developing Countries: The Limits of Conventional Economic Analysis." In *International Handbook on the Economics of Corruption*, edited by S. Rose-Ackerman. Cheltenham, UK, and Northampton, MA: Edward Elgar.

———. 2012. "Governance during Social Transformations: Challenges for Africa." *New Political Economy* 17 (5): 667–75.

Klitgaard, R. 1988. *Controlling Corruption*. Berkeley: University of California Press.

———. 2006. "Measuring Corruption in Eastern Europe and Central Asia: A Critique of the Cross-Country Indicators." Policy Research Working Paper no. 3968, World Bank, Washington, DC.

Knack, S. 2001. "Aid Dependence and the Quality of Governance: Cross-country Empirical Tests." *Southern Economic Journal* 68 (2): 310–29.

Knack, S., and A. Rahman. 2007. "Donor Fragmentation and Bureaucratic Quality in Aid Recipients." *Journal of Development Economics* 83 (1): 176–97.

Knutsen, C. H. 2013. "Democracy, State Capacity, and Economic Growth." *World Development* 43: 1–18.

Kolstad, I., and T. Søreide. 2009. "Corruption in Natural Resource Management: Implications for Policy Makers." *Resources Policy* 34: 214–26.

Kolstad, I., and A. Wiig. 2011. "Does Democracy Reduce Corruption?" CMI Working Paper no. 4:2011, Chr. Michelsen Institute, Bergen.

———. 2012. "What Determines Chinese Outward FDI?" *Journal of World Business* 47 (1): 26–34.

Kolstad, I., A. Wiig, and A. Williams. 2009. "Mission Improbable: Does Petroleum-related Aid Address the Resource Curse?" *Energy Policy* 37 (3): 954–65.

Kraakman, R. H. 1986. "Gatekeepers: The Anatomy of a Third-Party Enforcement Strategy." *Journal of Law, Economics and Organization* 2 (1): 53–104.

Kraay, A., and P. Murell. 2013. "Misunderstanding Corruption." Policy Research Working Paper no. 6488, World Bank, Washington, DC.

Krueger, A. O. 1974. "The Political Economy of the Rent-seeking Society." *American Economic Review* 64 (3): 291–303.

Kunicova, J. 2006. "Democratic Institutions and Corruption: Incentives and Constraints in Politics." In *International Handbook on the Economics of Corruption*, edited by S. Rose-Ackerman. Cheltenham, UK, and Northampton, MA: Edward Elgar.

Laffont, J. J. 2005. *Regulation and Development*. Cambridge: Cambridge University Press.

Laffont, J. J., and D. Martimort. 2001. *The Theory of Incentives: The Principal-Agent Model*. Princeton, NJ: Princeton University Press.

Laffont, J. J., and J. Tirole. 1991. "The Politics of Government Decision Making. A Theory of Regulatory Capture." *Quarterly Journal of Economics* 106 (4): 1089–127.

———. 1994. *A Theory of Incentives in Regulation and Procurement*. Cambridge, MA: MIT Press.

Lambert-Mogliansky, A. 2011. "Corruption and Collusion: Strategic Complements in Procurement." In *International Handbook on the Economics of Corruption*. Vol. 2, edited by S. Rose-Ackerman and T. Søreide. Cheltenham, UK, and Northampton, MA: Edward Elgar.

Lambsdorff, J. G. 2002a. "Making Corrupt Deals: Contracting in the Shadow of the Law." *Journal of Economic Behavior and Organization* 48 (3): 221–24.

———. 2002b. "Corruption and Rent-seeking." *Public Choice* 113 (1–2): 97–125.

———. 2006. "Consequences and Causes of Corruption: What Do We Know from a Cross-Section of Countries?" *International Handbook on the Economics of Corruption*, edited by S. Rose-Ackerman. Cheltenham, UK, and Northampton, MA: Edward Elgar.

———. 2007. *The Institutional Economics of Corruption and Reform: Theory, Evidence and Policy*. Cambridge: Cambridge University Press.

———. 2012. "Behaviorial and Experimental Economics as a Guide to Anticorruption." In *New Advances in Experimental Research on Corruption. Research in Experimental Economics*. Vol. 15, edited by S. Serra and L. Wantchekon. Bingley, UK: Emerald Insight.

Le Billon, P. 2012. *Wars of Plunder*. New York: Columbia University Press.

———. 2014. "Resource Grabs." In *Corruption, Grabbing and Development: Real World Challenges*, edited by T. Søreide and A. Williams. Cheltenham, UK, and Northampton, MA: Edward Elgar.

Leroy, A. M., and F. Fariello. 2012. *The World Bank Group Sanctions Process and Its Recent Reforms*. Washington, DC: World Bank.

Lindkvist, I. 2012. "Informal Payments and Health Worker Effort: A Quantitative Study from Tanzania." *Health Economics*. 22 (10): 1250–71.

———. 2014. "Using Salaries as a Deterrent to Informal Payments in the Health Sector." In *Corruption, Grabbing and Development: Real World Challenges*, edited by T. Søreide and A. Williams. Cheltenham, UK, and Northampton, MA: Edward Elgar.

Lui, F. 1985. "An Equilibrium Queuing Model of Bribery." *Journal of Political Economy* 93 (4): 760–81.

Mahdavy, H. 1970. "The Patterns and Problems of Economic Development in Rentier States: The Case of Iran." In *Studies in the Economic History of the Middle East*, edited by M. A. Cook. Oxford: Oxford University Press.

Mallaby, S. 2004. *The World's Banker*. New York: Penguin.

Manzetti, L. 1999. *Privatization South American Style*. New York: Oxford University Press.

McLeod, R. 2010. "Institutionalized Public Sector Corruption: A lecacy of the Suharto Franchise." In *The State and Illegality in Indonesia*, edited by E. Aspinall and G. van Klinken. Leiden: KITLV Press.

Mehlum, H., K. Moene, and R. Torvik. 2003. "Predator or Prey? Parasitic Enterprises in Economic Development." *European Economic Review* 47 (2): 275–94.

———. 2006. "Institutions and the Resource Curse." *Economic Journal* 116 (508): 1–20.

Méon, P. G., and K. Sekkat. 2005. "Does Corruption Grease or Sand the Wheels of Growth?" *Public Choice* 122 (1–2): 69–97.

Miceli, T. 2012. "Deterrence and Incapacitation Models of Criminal Punishment: Can the Twain Meet?" In *Research Handbook on the Economics of Criminal Law*, edited by A. Harel and K. N. Hylton. Cheltenham, UK, and Northampton, MA: Edward Elgar.

Miceli, M. P., J. P Near, and T. M. Dworkin. 2013. *Whistle-blowing in Organizations*. New York: Routledge.

Moody-Stuart, G. 1997. *How Business Bribes Damage Developing Countries*. Tampa: World View.

Mookherjee, B., and I. P. L. Png. 1992. "Monitoring vis-à-vis Investigation in Enforcement of Law." *American Economic Review* 82 (3): 556–65.

Moore, M. S. 2010. *Placing Blame: A Theory of the Criminal Law*. Oxford University Press.

Morrison, K. M. 2012. "What Can We Learn about the 'Resource Curse' from Foreign Aid?" *World Bank Research Observer* 27 (1): 52–73.

Motta, M. 2004. *Competition Policy: Theory and Practice*. Cambridge: Cambridge University Press.

Motta, M., and M. Polo. 2003. "Leniency Programs and Cartel Prosecution." *International Journal of Industrial Organization* 21: 347–79.

Mueller, D. C. 2003. *Public Choice III*. Cambridge: Cambridge University Press.

Musila, J., and S. Sigué. 2010. "Corruption and International Trade: An Empirical Investigation of African Countries." *The World Economy* 33 (1): 129–46.

Ndikumana, L., and J. Boyce. 2011. *Africa's Odious Debts: How Foreign Loans and Capital Flight Bled a Continent*. London: Zed.

Nordhaus, W. D. 1975. "The Political Business Cycle." *Review of Economic Studies* 42 (2): 169–90.

NOU (Norwegian Official Reports). 2009. *Tax Havens and Development*. Report from the Government Commission on Capital Flight from Poor Countries. Official Norwegian Reports 2009:19, Oslo: Ministry of Foreign Affairs.

Oded, S. 2011. "Inducing Corporate Compliance: A Compound Corporate Liability Regime." *International Review of Law and Economics* 31 (4): 272–83.

Olken, B. 2007. "Monitoring Corruption: Evidence from a Field Experiment in Indonesia." *Journal of Political Economy* 115 (2): 200–49.

Olson, M. 1996. "Big Bills Left on the Sidewalk: Why Some Nations are Rich, and Others Poor." *Journal of Economic Perspectives* 10 (2): 3–24.

Ostrom, E. 2000. "Collective Action and the Evolution of Social Norms." *Journal of Economic Perspectives* 14 (3): 137–58.

Oubda, F. 2013. "Public Expenditure Tracking Survey in Burkina Faso. Reducing Leakages and Improving Information Systems in the Education Sector." In *IIEP Newsletter*, No. 2. Paris: IIEP-UNESCO.

Page, J. 2008. "Rowing Against the Current. The Diversification Challenge in Africa's Resource Rich Countries." Working Paper no. 29, Brookings Institution, Global Economy and Development Program, Washington, DC.

Park, S., and F. Berry. 2012. "Successful Diffusion of a Failed Policy: The Case of Pay-for-Performance in the US Federal Government." *Public Management Review* 16 (6): 1–19.

Pashev, K., N. Valev, and V. Pasheva. 2010. "Corruption in the Tax Administration: Is There Scope for Wage Incentives?" Working Paper No. 1023, International Center for Public Policy, Andrew Young School of Policy Studies, Georgia.

Peisakhin, L. V. 2011. "Field Experimentation and the Study of Corruption." In *The International Handbook on the Economics of Corruption*. Vol. 2, edited by S. Rose-Ackerman and T. Søreide. Cheltenham, UK, and Northampton, MA: Edward Elgar.

Persson, T., and G. Tabellini. 2000. *Political Economics*. Cambridge, MA: MIT Press.

Piga, G. 2011. "A Fighting Chance against Corruption in Public Procurement." In *The International Handbook on the Economics of Corruption*. Vol. 2, edited by S. Rose-Ackerman and T. Søreide. Cheltenham, UK, and Northampton, MA: Edward Elgar.

Pincus, J. R., and J. A. Winters, eds. 2003. *Reinventing the World Bank*. Ithaca, NY: Cornell University Press.

Pink, D. H. 2010. *Drive: The Surprising Truth about What Motivates Us*. New York: Canongate.

Pinker, S. 1997. *How the Mind Works*. New York: W. W. Norton.

Piselli, E. 2000. "The Scope for Excluding Providers Who Have Committed Criminal Offences under the E. U. Procurement Directives." *Public Procurement Law Review* 9: 267–86.

Poate, D., and C. Vaillant. 2011. *Joint Evaluation of Support to Anti-Corruption Efforts Synthesis 2002–2009*. Financed by Several Donor Agencies. http://www.norad.no/en/tools-and-publications/publications/publication?key=384730.

Poisson, M. 2014. "Grabbing in the Education Sector." In *Corruption, Grabbing and Development: Real World Challenges*, edited by T. Søreide and A. Williams. Cheltenham, UK, and Northampton, MA: Edward Elgar.

Puntillo, R. 1996. "Mass Privatization in Poland and Russia: The Case of the Tortoise and the Hare?" *Journal of Emerging Markets* 1 (1): 7–28.

Raballand, G., and J. F. Marteu. 2014. "Rents Extraction in the Sub-Saharan Africa Port Sector." In *Corruption, Grabbing and Development: Real World Challenges*, edited by T. Søreide and A. Williams. Cheltenham, UK, and Northampton, MA: Edward Elgar.

Rabl, T., and T. M. Kühlmann. 2009. "Why or Why Not? Rationalizing Corruption in Organizations." *Cross Cultural Management* 16 (3): 268–86.

Rauch, J. E., and Evans, P. B. 2000. "Bureaucratic Structure and Bureaucratic Performance in Less Developed Countries." *Journal of Public Economics* 75 (1): 49–71.

Ravallion, M. 2009. "Evaluation in the Practice of Development." *World Bank Research Observer* 24 (1): 30–53.

Razafindrakato, M., and F. Roubaud. 2010. "Are International Databases on Corruption Reliable? A Comparison of Expert Opinion Surveys and Household Surveys in Sub-Saharan Africa." *World Development* 38 (8): 1057–69.

Recanatini, F. 2011. "Anticorruption Authorities: An Effective Tool to Curb Corruption?" In *International Handbook on the Economics of Corruption*. Vol. 2, edited by S. Rose-Ackerman and T. Søreide. Cheltenham, UK, and Northampton, MA: Edward Elgar.

Reed, Q., and A. Fontana. 2011. "Corruption and Illicit Financial Flows: The Limits and Possibilities of Current Approaches." U4 Issue Paper no. 2:2011, U4 Anticorruption Resource Center, Chr. Michelsen Institute, Bergen.

Reinikka, R., and J. Svensson. 2004. "Local Capture: Evidence from a Central Government Transfer Program in Uganda." *Quarterly Journal of Economics* 119 (2): 679–705.

———. 2006. "Using Micro-Surveys to Measure and Explain Corruption." *World Development* 34 (2): 359–70.

Reuter, P., ed. 2012. *Draining Development?: Controlling Flows of Illicit Funds from Developing Countries*. Washington, DC: World Bank Publications.

Rivas, M. F. 2008. "An Experiment on Corruption and Gender." The Paper no. 08/10, Department of Economic Theory and Economic History, University of Granada.

Robinson, J. A., R. Torvik, and T. Verdier. 2006. "Political Foundations of the Resource Curse." *Journal of Development Economics* 79 (2): 447–68.

Rock, M. 2009. "Corruption and Democracy." *Journal of Development Studies* 45 (1): 55–75.

Rose, J., and P. M. Heywood. 2013. "Political Science Approaches to Integrity and Corruption." *Human Affairs* 23 (2): 148–59.

Rose-Ackerman, S. 1978. *Corruption: A Study in Political Economy*. New York: Academic.

———. 1999. *Corruption and Government. Causes, Consequences and Reform*. Cambridge: Cambridge University Press.

———. 2001. "Trust, Honesty, and Corruption: Reflection on the State-Building Process." *European Journal of Sociology* 42 (3): 526–70.

———. 2010a. "The Law and Economics of Bribery and Extortion." *Annual Review of Law and Social Science* 6: 217–36.

———. 2010b. "Corruption: Greed, Culture, and the State." *Yale Law Journal Online* 120: 125–40.

———. 2013. "Introduction: The Role of International Actors in Fighting Corruption." In *Anticorruption Policy: Can International Actors Play a Constructive Role?* edited by S. Rose-Ackerman and P. Carrington. Durham, NC: Carolina Academic Press.

Rose-Ackerman, S., and P. Carrington, eds. 2013. *Anticorruption Policy: Can International Actors Play a Constructive Role?* Durham, NC: Carolina Academic Press.

Rose-Ackerman, S., and T. Søreide, eds. 2011. *The International Handbook on the Economics of Corruption*. Vol. Two. Cheltenham UK and Northampton, MA. Edward Elgar Publishing.

Rose-Ackerman, S., and R. Truex. 2013. "Corruption and Policy Reform." In *Global Problems, Smart Solutions: Costs and Benefits*, edited by B. Lomborg. Cambridge: Cambridge University Press.

Rothstein, B., and J. Teorell. 2008. "What Is Quality of Goverment? A Theory of Impartial Government Institutions." *Governance: An International Journal of Policy, Administration and Institutions* 21: 165–90.

Rousseau, J. J. (1762) 2004. *The Social Contract*. Penguin.

Sabet, D. 2012. "Understanding the Padma Bridge Controversy." Monthly Current Events Analysis Series, prepared for the Center for Enterprise and Society, University of Liberal Arts, Bangladesh.

Salvatore, D. 2003. *Microeconomics: Theory and Applications*. 4th ed. Oxford: Oxford University Press.

Sandholtz, W., and R. Taagepera. 2005. "Corruption, Culture, and Communism." *International Review of Sociology* 15 (1): 109–31.

Sanghi, A., D. Hankinson, and A. Sundakov. 2007. *Designing and Using Public-Private Partnership Units in Infrastructure: Lessons from Case Studies around the World*. Washington, DC: World Bank.

Scanteam. 2013. "Facing the Resource Curse: Norway's Oil for Development Program." Norad Evaluation Report no. 6/2012, Norad, Oslo.

Schikora, J. T. 2011. "Bringing Good and Bad Whistle-blowers to the Lab." Münchener Wirtschaftswissenschaftliche Beiträge (VWL), Report no. 2011–4. Ludwig-Maximilians-Universität München, Munich.

Schooner, S. L. 2004. "The Paper Tiger Stirs: Rethinking Suspension and Debarment." *Public Procurement Law Review* 5: 211–17.

Schulze, G. G., and B. Frank. 2003. "Deterrence versus Intrinsic Motivation: Experimental Evidence on the Determinants of Corruptibility." *Economics of Governance* 4 (2): 143–60.

Schultz, J., and T. Søreide. 2008. "Corruption in Emergency Procurement." *Disasters Journal* 32 (4): 516–36.

Seiler, N., and J. Madir. 2012. "Fight against Corruption: Sanctions Regimes of Multilateral Development Banks." *Journal of International Economic Law* 15 (1): 5–28.

Sequeira, S., and S. Djankov. 2010. "An Empirical Study of Corruption in Ports." Draft paper available at Social Science Research Network, SSRN no. 1589066. http://ssrn.com/abstract=1589066.

Serra, D., and L. Wantchekon, eds. 2012. *New Advances in Experimental Research on Corruption: Research in Experimental Economics*. Bingley, UK: Emerald Books.

Shafir, E., ed. 2013. *The Behavioral Foundations for Public Policy*. Princeton, NJ: Princeton University Press.

Sharman, J. C., 2010. "Shopping for Anonymous Shell Companies: An Audit Study of Anonymity and Crime in the International Financial System." *Journal of Economic Perspectives* 24 (4): 127–40.

———. 2012. "Chasing Kleptocrats' Loot: Narrowing the Effectiveness Gap." U4 Issue Paper no. 4:2012, U4 Anticorruption Resource Center, Chr. Michelsen Institute, Bergen.

Shaxson, N. 2011. *Treasure Islands: Tax Havens and the Men Who Stole the World*. London: Bodley Head.

Shleifer, A., and R. W. Vishny. 1993. "Corruption." *Quarterly Journal of Economics* 108 (3): 599–617.

———. 2002. *The Grabbing Hand: Government Pathologies and Their Cures*. Cambridge, MA: Harvard University Press.

Skage, I. A., T. Søreide, and A. Tostensen. 2014. "When Per Diems Take Over: Training and Travel as Extra Pay." In *Corruption, Grabbing and Development: Real World Challenges*, edited by T. Søreide and A. Williams. Cheltenham, UK, and Northampton, MA: Edward Elgar.

Skaperdas, S. 2001. "The Political Economy of Organized Crime: Providing Protection When the State Does Not." *Economics of Governance* 2 (3): 173–202.

Smith, D. J. 2003. "Patronage, Per Diems and the 'Workshop Mentality': The Practice of Family Planning Programs in Southeastern Nigeria." *World Development* 31 (4): 703–15.

Søreide, T. 2006. "Is It Right/Wrong to Rank?" Paper presented to "IV Global Forum on Fighting Corruption and Safeguarding Integrity," Session Measuring Integrity, Brasilia, Released as a CMI working paper, Chr. Michelsen Institute, Bergen.

———. 2008. "Beaten by Bribery: Why Not Blow the Whistle?" *Journal of Institutional and Theoretical Economics* 164 (3): 407–28.

———. 2009. "Too Risk Averse to Stay Honest? Business Corruption, Uncertainty and Attitudes toward Risk." *International Review of Law and Economics* 2009 (29): 388–95.

———. 2011. "The Governance of Infrastructure Regulation: An Economist's View." In *Emerging Issues in Competition, Collusion, and Regulation of Network Industries*, edited by A. Estache. London: Centre for Economic Policy Research.

———. 2012. "Risks of Corruption and Collusion in Regulated Sectors: Study Note on the Closure of Markets and Other Dysfunctions in the Award of Concessions Contracts." The European Parliament Committee on Internal Market and Consumer Protection, IP/A/IMCO/NT/2012-10.

———. 2013. "Democracy's Shortcomings in Anti-corruption." In *Anti-Corruption Policy: Can International Actors Play a Constructive Role?* edited by S. Rose-Ackerman and P. Carrington. Durham, NC: Carolina Academic Press.

Søreide, T., A. Tostensen, and I. A. Skage. 2012. "Hunting for Per Diem: The Uses and Abuses of Travel Compensation in Three Developing Countries." Norad Report no. 2/2012, Norad, Oslo.

Søreide, T., and R. Truex. 2013. "Multistakeholder Groups for Better Sector Performance: A Key to Fight Corruption in Natural Resource Governance?" *Development Policy Review* 31 (2): 203–17.

Søreide, T., and A. Williams. 2014. *Corruption, Grabbing and Development: Real World Challenges*. Cheltenham, UK, and Northampton, MA: Edward Elgar.

Spagnolo, G. 2004. "Divide et Impera: Optimal Leniency Programs. Discussion Paper no. 4840, Centre for Economic Policy Research, London.

———. 2006. "Leniency and Whistleblowers in Antitrust." Discussion Paper no. 5794, Centre for Economic Policy Research, London.

Stansbury, N. 2005. "Exposing the Foundations of Corruption in Construction." In *Global Corruption Report*. Berlin: Transparency International.

Svensson, J. 2000a. "Foreign Aid and Rent-seeking." *Journal of International Economics* 51 (2): 437–61.

———. 2000b. "When Is Foreign Aid Policy Credible? Aid Dependence and Conditionality." *Journal of Development Economics* 61 (1): 61–84.

———. 2003. "Who Must Pay Bribes and How Much? Evidence from a Cross Section of Firms." *Quarterly Journal of Economics* 118 (1): 207–30.

———. 2005. "Eight Questions about Corruption." *Journal of Economic Perspectives* 19 (3): 19–42.

Swamy, A., S. Knack, Y. Lee, and O. Azfar. 2001. "Gender and Corruption." *Journal of Development Economics* 64 (1): 25–55.

Tirole, J. 1986. "Hierarchies and Bureaucracies: On the Role of Collusion in Organizations." *Journal of Economics and Organization* 2 (2): 181–214.

———. 1996. "A Theory of Collective Reputations (with Applications to the Persistence of Corruption and to Firm Quality)." *Review of Economic Studies* 63 (1): 1–22.

Tollison, R. D. 1982. "Rent Seeking: A Survey." *Kyklos* 35 (4): 575–602.

Torgler, B., and N. Valev. 2010. "Gender and Public Attitudes toward Corruption and Tax Evasion." *Contemporary Economic Policy* 28 (4): 554–68.

Torvik, R. 2009. "Why Do Some Resource-abundant Countries Succeed While Others Do Not?" *Oxford Review of Economic Policy* 25 (2): 241–56.

Transparency International. 2012. *Money, Politics, Power: Corruption Risks in Europe*. Berlin: Transparency International.

———. 2013. "Exporting Corruption? Progress Report 2013: Assessing Enforcement of the OECD Convention on Combating Foreign Bribery." Transparency International, Berlin.

Treisman, D. 2000. "The Causes of Corruption: A Cross-National Study." *Journal of Public Economics* 76 (3): 399–457.

———. 2007. "What Have We Learned about the Causes of Corruption from Ten Years of Cross-National Empirical Research?" *Annual Review of Political Science* 10: 211–44.

Trivers, R. 1971. "The Evolution of Reciprocal Altruism." *Quarterly Review of Biology* 46: 35–57.

Trongmateerut, P., and J. T. Sweeney. 2013. "The Influence of Subjective Norms on Whistle-Blowing: A Cross-Cultural Investigation." *Journal of Business Ethics* 112 (3): 437–51.

Truex, R., and T. Søreide. 2011. "Why Multistakeholder Groups Succeed and Fail." In *The International Handbook on the Economics of Corruption*. Vol. 2, edited by S. Rose-Ackerman and T. Søreide. Cheltenham, UK, and Northampton, MA: Edward Elgar.

Tullock, G. 2005. *The Rent-Seeking Society: The Selected Works of Gordon Tullock*. Vol. 5, edited by Charles K. Rowley. Indianapolis, IN: Liberty Fund.

Underkuffler, L. S. 2013. *Captured by Evil: The Idea of Corruption in Law*. New Haven, CT: Yale University Press.

United Nations Development Programme (UNDP). 2011. *Fighting Corruption in the Education Sector. Methods, Tools and Good Practices*. New York: UNDP.

Vandenabeele, W. 2007. "Toward a Public Administration Theory of Public Service Motivation: An Institutional Approach." *Public Management Review* 9 (4): 545–56.

Vannucci, A. 2009. "The Controversial Legacy of 'Mani Pulite': A Critical Analysis of Italian Corruption and Anticorruption Policies." *Bulletin of Italian Politics* 1 (2): 233–64.

Van Rijckeghem, C., and B. Weder. 2001. "Bureaucratic Corruption and the Rate of Temptation: How Much Do Wages in the Civil Service Affect Corruption?" *Journal of Development Economics* 65 (2): 307–31.

Van Winden, F., and A. Ash. 2009. "On the Behavioral Economics of Crime." Paper prepared for the workshop "Beyond the Economics of Crime," Heidelberg, March 19–21.

Varian, H. 1992. *Microeconomic Analysis*. 3rd ed. New York: W.W Norton.

Vian, T., K. Gryboski, Z. Sinoimeric, and R. Hall. 2006. "Informal Payments in Government Health Facilities in Albania: Results of a Qualitative Study." *Social Science and Medicine* 62 (4): 877–87.

Vicente, P. 2010. "Does Oil Corrupt? Evidence from a Natural Experiment in West Africa." *Journal of Development Economics* 92 (1): 28–38.

———. 2011. "Oil, Corruption and Vote-buying: A Review of the Case of São Tomé and Princípe." In *International Handbook on the Economics of Corruption*. Vol. 2, edited by S. Rose-Ackerman and T. Søreide. Cheltenham, UK, and Northampton, MA: Edward Elgar.

Wantchekon, L. 2003. "Clientelism and Voting Behavior: Evidence from a Field Experiment in Benin." *World Politics* 55 (3): 399–422.

Wayne, S., and R. Taagepera. 2005. "Corruption, Culture and Communism." *International Review of Sociology* 15 (1): 109–31.

Weibel, A., K. Rost, and M. Ostreloch. 2010. "Pay for Performance in the Public Sector: Benefits and (Hidden) Costs." *Journal of Public Administration and Management* 20 (2): 387–412.

Weitz-Shapiro, R., and M. S. Winters. 2010. "Lacking Information or Condoning Corruption. Voter Attitudes toward Corruption in Brazil." Paper presented at the American Political Science Association annual meeting, Washington, DC.

Wells, J. 2014. "Corruption and Collusion in Construction: A View from the Industry." In *Corruption, Grabbing and Development: Real World Challenges*, edited by T. Søreide and A. Williams. Cheltenham, UK, and Northampton, MA: Edward Elgar.

Williams, S. 2006. "The Mandatory Exclusion for Corruption in the New EC Procurement Directives." *European Law Review* 31 (5): 711–34.

———. 2009. "Coordinating Public Procurement to Support EU Objectives—A First Step? The Case of Exclusions for Serious Criminal Offences." In *Social and Environmental Policies in EC Procurement Law*, edited by S. Arrowsmith and P. Kunzlik. Cambridge: Cambridge University Press.

World Bank. 2012. *World Bank Legal Review: International Financial Institutions and Global Legal Governance*. Vol. 3, edited by H. Cisse, D. D. Bradlow and B. Kingsbury. Law, Justice and Development Series. Washington, DC: World Bank.

Wren-Lewis, L. 2013. "Do Infrastructure Reforms Reduce the Effect of Corruption? Theory and Evidence from Latin America and the Caribbean." Policy Research Working Paper no. 6559, World Bank, Washington, DC.

Environmental Benefits Statement

The World Bank is committed to reducing its environmental footprint. In support of this commitment, the Publishing and Knowledge Division leverages electronic publishing options and print-on-demand technology, which is located in regional hubs worldwide. Together, these initiatives enable print runs to be lowered and shipping distances decreased, resulting in reduced paper consumption, chemical use, greenhouse gas emissions, and waste.

The Publishing and Knowledge Division follows the recommended standards for paper use set by the Green Press Initiative. Whenever possible, books are printed on 50 percent to 100 percent postconsumer recycled paper, and at least 50 percent of the fiber in our book paper is either unbleached or bleached using Totally Chlorine Free (TCF), Processed Chlorine Free (PCF), or Enhanced Elemental Chlorine Free (EECF) processes.

More information about the Bank's environmental philosophy can be found at http://crinfo.worldbank.org/wbcrinfo/node/4.

green press
INITIATIVE